How to Manage with NLP

Books that make you better

Books that make you better. That make you *be* better, *do* better, *feel* better. Whether you want to upgrade your personal skills or change your job, whether you want to improve your managerial style, become a more powerful communicator, or be stimulated and inspired as you work.

Prentice Hall Business is leading the field with a new breed of skills, careers and development books. Books that are a cut above the mainstream – in topic, content and delivery – with an edge and verve that will make you better, with less effort.

Books that are as sharp and smart as you are.

Prentice Hall Business
We work harder – so you don't have to.

For more details on products, and to contact us, visit
www.pearsoned.co.uk

How to Manage with NLP

3rd edition

David Molden

**Prentice Hall
Business
is an imprint of**

Harlow, England • London • New York • Boston • San Francisco • Toronto • Sydney • Singapore • Hong Kong
Tokyo • Seoul • Taipei • New Delhi • Cape Town • Madrid • Mexico City • Amsterdam • Munich • Paris • Milan

PEARSON EDUCATION LIMITED

Edinburgh Gate
Harlow CM20 2JE
Tel: +44 (0)1279 623623
Fax: +44 (0)1279 431059
Website: www.pearsoned.co.uk

First published in Great Britain in 1996 as *Managing with the Power of NLP*
Second edition 2007
Third edition 2011, published as *How to Manage with NLP*

Pearson Education is not responsible for the content of third party internet sites.

ISBN: 978-0-273-74566-2

British Library Cataloguing-in-Publication Data
A catalogue record for this book is available from the British Library

Library of Congress Cataloging-in-Publication Data
A catalog record for this book is available from the Library of Congress

10 9 8 7 6 5 4 3 2 1
15 14 13 12 11

Typeset in 10/15pt Iowan Old Style BT by 3
Printed by Ashford Colour Press, Gosport

Contents

About the author   *vi*

Acknowledgements   *vii*

Introduction   1

01 How good a manager are you?   5

02 From ideas to action   25

03 Creating direction   49

04 Self-mastery   67

05 Power to the people   91

06 Exploring your mind   113

07 The power of words   135

08 Influence and persuasion   161

09 Applying NLP to 10 everyday challenges   179

Notes   247

Index   249

About the author

David Molden is a director, coach and trainer with Quadrant 1 International, a company set up to help business people aspire, create, lead and succeed. David's assignments include 1:1 coaching of clients and a range of projects with large corporations, small businesses and entrepreneurs. He is also a key trainer on NLP Business Practitioner Courses run in the UK by Quadrant 1 and internationally through partner organisations.

David gained valuable management experience in the IT sector where he learned how to succeed through motivating individuals and teams. He found the experience so personally rewarding that he left his role as head of service, training and development with Computacenter plc to invest in his own skills and reshape his career to do what he enjoys most – helping people to unleash their full potential.

Today he works with business teams, CEOs and managers across a variety of sectors and in many different countries. He is a senior partner with the Oxford Taiji Gongfu Institute, a Tai Chi instructor and a personal student of Grandmaster Gou Kongjie, 11th generation Chen style. He has authored and co-authored a number of NLP books which have been translated into more than 15 languages. He lives in Oxford, and enjoys travelling, writing, music, Tai Chi and reading. He has a particular interest in eastern wisdom and its applications in the modern world.

Acknowledgements

To the two pioneers and originators of NLP – Richard Bandler and John Grinder – and to the many people responsible for the multitude of developments and applications. To all my teachers, especially Brad Waldron, Willie Monteiro, Wyatt Woodsmall and Marvin Oka. To Robert Dilts for his work on neurological levels, his insights into belief structures and his modelling of Walt Disney and Albert Einstein. To my co-director and co-author Pat Hutchinson who has generously given her time to help shape the book. To the many contributors to the field of NLP, far too many to mention, and finally but most importantly to the many clients of Quadrant 1 International who have helped us all learn so much along the way.

Introduction

Vividly planted in my memory is the day I became a manager and acquired the responsibility for hiring and firing and for the performance of people. Some of these people I had recruited, others were hired by my predecessor, and some were from my previous peer group. I was also expected to be a salesman and win contracts, to give customer presentations, to represent my business unit at company conferences and to take responsibility for a significant budget. I was also expected to fix a range of problems which were having an impact on profitability.

Looking back on those early days, I realise how much easier it might have been had NLP been available to me. What I did have was a very effective CEO and chairman team from whom I learned many lessons, and I was also able to observe and learn from a number of directors, some of whom seemed to achieve excellent results and others who did not. It is my experience as an ambitious manager in the IT services industry that I have used as my inspiration and drive to write this book, so that managers today have the most up-to-date and effective tools available to help them succeed.

If you are inspired to look beyond conventional teaching models for *new* ways of developing management competence, this book is written for you. It concentrates on *you*, the manager, and how *you* can change to develop greater degrees of excellence.

NLP means neurolinguistic programming ...

Neuro – how you use your brain

Linguistic – verbal and non-verbal language you use to organise your thoughts and communicate with others and with yourself

Programming – the unique way you create programmes which drive your behaviour.

Whatever your experience, status, role or objectives, NLP provides you with the learning to develop your fullest potential and realise success in management through fast, flexible, generative techniques.

Generative development

The manager's role can be defined using a 'generative management development' model. The concept behind the model is simple. You operate within three core management dimensions – leadership, communication and innovation (refer to Figure 0.1). The term *generative* means that, unlike other more conventional types of learning, when you have a strategy for continual learning then new skills come out of your everyday experiences – so learning is generated as an ongoing process, rather than something you reserve for the classroom.

You operate in the organisation as a leader, communicator and innovator. You get feedback from your efforts in each of these

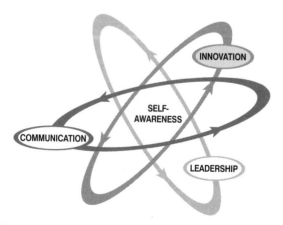

Figure 0.1 Generative management development model

three dimensions, which you can choose either to ignore or to learn from. Should you choose to take notice of your feedback you can use it to make changes to your behaviour. For example, if a meeting isn't going the way you had intended it to go, what are you learning about the way you have been interacting? Have you been communicating clearly? Have you demonstrated leadership? Were you curious enough to know more about the situation? What can you do differently to improve things?

Spending time noticing your feedback and making intelligent choices in the three dimensions of leadership, communication and innovation will improve self-awareness and enhance personal development. In this way the model is generative, which means that you are constantly generating your own learning and development in all *four* key dimensions:

1 **Self-awareness**. How well you know yourself; what makes you tick; creating direction and setting outcomes for yourself; being a role model and improving your capability to integrate new learning.

2 **Leadership**. How you organise yourself and the methods you use to motivate, direct, develop and get the most from yourself and your team. What behaviours you are role modelling for others. What others are learning from your leadership.

3 **Communication**. How you connect with yourself and engage with others at both a mental and emotional level.

4 **Innovation**. How you provide variety, create a platform for new ideas and foster an environment of learning and innovation.

Getting the most from this book

The first time you try something completely new you may feel awkward. You can test this awkwardness very simply by putting your wristwatch on the opposite wrist, or your ring on a different finger, or writing with the opposite hand you usually write with. If you are able to push through the awkward feelings over time you will begin to feel increasingly more comfortable. This is the approach you need for the practical exercises in this book, which will present you with many new ways of thinking and being. Practise, push through any awkwardness and get NLP into the muscle. If you can do this you will reap many personal and business benefits.

"Chaos often breeds life, when order breeds habit."
Henry B. Adams (1838–1918), American historian

01

How good a manager are you?

Your autopilot – is it working for or against you?

How often are you 'preoccupied' in your thoughts? How many times, while driving home from work, have you caught yourself running a movie in your mind of some incident earlier in the day – and upon arriving home you're unable to recall the journey?

"The chains of habit are too weak to be felt until they are too strong to be broken."

Dr Samuel Johnson (1709–84), British poet and author

In order to carry out this review activity you have to hand over the act of 'driving' to your autopilot so your conscious attention can be focused inward. It is no coincidence that we call this process 'reflection'.

From this example we can extract three learning points.

1 We are very adept at repeating a process once we have learned how to do it (driving). Once habits are formed they are maintained extremely well by unconscious processing (autopilot).

2 New habits can be difficult to break, especially as you have to consciously think about the habit in order to avoid doing it. Have you ever tried driving an automatic car for the first time and found yourself fumbling for the clutch and gearstick?

3 Change often requires 'unlearning' unwanted habits before learning more useful ones. Car drivers can become dangerous through the habits they develop – like driving too close to the car in front.

Is your autopilot working for you or against you? To answer this question, a little self-analysis may help you to learn precisely *how* you communicate with yourself and *how* you programme your autopilot to learn new habits. Let's begin by taking a look at the way you respond to problems.

> **Thinking in negatives – what can't be done or what isn't possible – acts on the unconscious as a limiting and disempowering influence.**

How do you respond to problems?

Here's a question for you to contemplate: *Can you fit a square peg into a round hole?* What kind of answers would you expect?

1 **No – it can't be done.** This is the response of a *defeatist*, reacting to a situation as presented and concluding with the word *can't*. It communicates a message of inflexibility and self-doubt, causing you to focus on the impossible rather than the possible. The word is also untrue in many contexts where it is used. How do you know it can't be done?

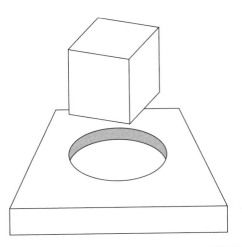

> **Take the *t* out of *can't*! Instead, think what can be done and what is possible.**

A more truthful response might be *I haven't yet found a way of doing that*. In a commercial environment customers are not interested in what you *can't* do for them – they want to know what you *can* do, and yes, sometimes they will ask for what seems like the impossible. It is often when you are exploring the seemingly impossible that new and more creative alternatives emerge.

2 **Give me a big enough mallet and I'll try**. This is the response of a *reactionary*. It demonstrates a determination to direct energy into one reactive solution. As a consequence the peg, hole and mallet are all likely to be damaged.

3 **Yes – if I reshape the square peg so that it fits**. This is a *complex* response. For the peg to fit I must learn how to reshape square pegs into round ones. It is complex because the consequences are often redesigns to systems, processes and procedures or restructures that are often inappropriate or unworkable. It is also reactionary as it is reacting to the situation as presented without question.

4 **What would be the purpose for the fit and how did a square peg ever come to be offered to a round hole in the first place?** This is a *curious* response. It seeks to identify the intention behind the question, looking for more information outside of the frame presented. The result is a clearer picture of the situation with which to aid a decision-making process. This response challenges the question, i.e. it does not presuppose that the objective is to fit a square peg into a round hole. It's not that everything should be challenged, but by not challenging there is a possibility that your business will get stuck in outmoded ways of operating.

Some years ago, a friend of mine was approached by his director with a plan for developing a central IT support facility to cover the UK. He was delighted at having been given a strategic project to manage and accepted all the presuppositions that came with it, including – *that UK analysts wanted a centralised support facility.* Unbeknown to him this was a square peg in a round hole situation.

Three years later the support facility was in a confused mess. It had a reputation for poor service, the management team disagreed about the basic purpose of the department and it was costing far too much to maintain. There had been changes to systems and investment in new technology to try to make it work. The UK analysts who were the clients of the service had never been consulted, and they could see little benefit in the investment. They preferred local support groups because they liked to network with their peers. This situation could possibly have been avoided if the presuppositions contained in the original brief had been challenged. The support group was eventually broken up and dissolved.

Challenging presuppositions helps to make sense of seemingly ambiguous situations.

The curiosity response needs flexibility of thinking, being open to discover something new or different about the situation. Being flexible means having an attitude of mind that produces desired results regardless of the present situation, its complexities, ambiguities, pace, expectations, culture and presuppositions. In systems theory[1] – which has much in common with NLP's holistic approach to learning and change – there is a principle called the *law of requisite variety* which states that 'in order to successfully adapt and survive, a member of a system needs a certain amount of flexibility, and that flexibility has to be proportional to the potential variation or uncertainty in the rest of the system'. For managers this means never being content with one solution, but instead challenging presuppositions, looking at influences in the wider system of the organisation and generating as many alternative courses of action as you need to create new effective possibilities.

NLP

In order to successfully adapt and survive, a member of a system needs a certain amount of flexibility, and that flexibility has to be proportional to the potential variation or the uncertainty in the rest of the system.

Whenever you are faced with a challenge, you will have four basic choices of response:

1 Defeat

2 Reaction

3 Complexity

4 Curiosity.

The flexible manager will begin with option 4 as a default.

What do you believe you are managing?

You have read how habits of thinking and language can create limitations. You will focus on what you believe is important. You will manage what you believe you are there to manage. Your personal values will influence your actions, and how you see yourself will determine how successful you will be. Your beliefs, your values and your sense of higher purpose as a manager act upon each other and create your behaviour. How this works can be explained using a simple model.

There are five levels of learning, communication and change[2] that are key to developing your flexibility of thinking and behaviour. The five levels are as follows:

1 Identity or role

2 Values and beliefs

3 Capabilities

4 Behaviour

5 Environment.

Figure 1.1 shows these levels within a contextual frame. The context, or situation you are in, will influence each of these levels: so, for example, you may base your behaviour on one set of values and beliefs when at work and on a different set at home; what you value as a parent may be very different from what you value as a manager. How you act with your boss may be different from how you act with a customer. Sometimes the difference between these levels provides an insight into poor performance.

Identity – *who?*

People who make career moves start by reframing their identity. They often don't think of it in this way at all – people rarely wake up in the morning and say 'I've decided to change my identity', but that's what actually happens. Take a few moments to think about your professional identity and complete this statement: 'I am …' The words you use to describe yourself are labels for your identity.

Labels put meaning to things and influence how we think about them – for example, project leader, head of finance, personnel officer, etc. One retail company we have been working with has chosen to call all its employees at every level 'colleagues' to help move away from a status-centred and hierarchical culture. Their business cards only tell you which part of the business they represent, not the role they perform.

The words you use to describe and think about your roles can greatly influence what you do to fulfil each role.

Identity labels greatly influence your autopilot and it is here, at the level of identity, that you can make significant changes to your performance.

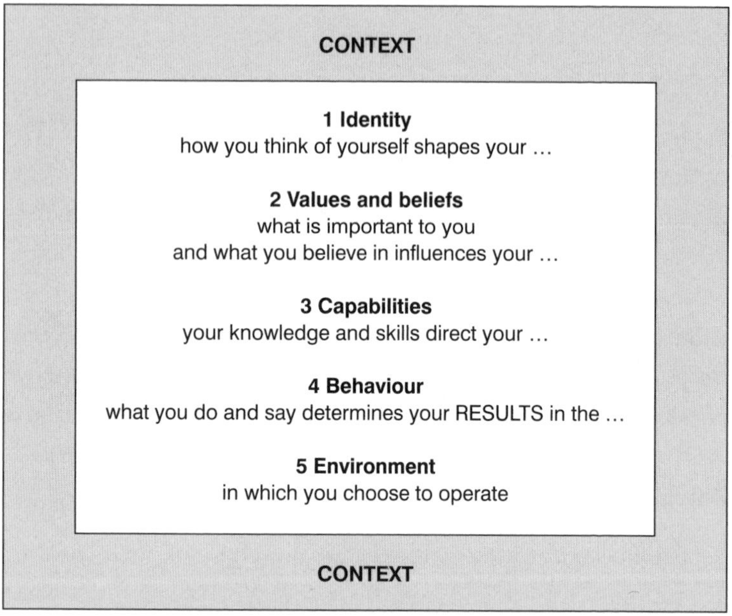

CONTEXT

1 Identity
how you think of yourself shapes your …

2 Values and beliefs
what is important to you
and what you believe in influences your …

3 Capabilities
your knowledge and skills direct your …

4 Behaviour
what you do and say determines your RESULTS in the …

5 Environment
in which you choose to operate

CONTEXT

Figure 1.1 Levels of learning, communication and change

Exercise 1.1: Identify with your role

The objective is for you to think of the labels you currently apply to your professional roles and consider whether there may be more appropriate labels that will help you to be more flexible and successful in those roles.

On the left-hand side of Table 1 write one label per line for each of your professional roles. Then for each label in turn, run a movie in your mind of a specific time when you were performing this role. Become fully connected with this situation and make the movie vivid by fully concentrating on it … make it a bright, colourful, moving 3-D picture … add surround sound so that you can hear the words of the conversations you are having … and when you are fully connected with this experience, … notice what you say and do, and if you notice parts of your movie that cause you to feel uncomfortable, ask yourself: *What's going on here*? And then ask yourself these questions: *How could I have been even more flexible in my approach to this situation? What could I change in order to improve my results here*?

For example, imagine you are the manager in charge of a helpdesk and you identify one of your role labels as an 'information organiser'. As you connect with a typical day, you may focus on collecting and filing information logged from your customers using time that could perhaps be better utilised to reduce the customer's dependency on your service. A more useful role label might be 'educator'. This exercise will generate some different labels for each of your roles. Write these labels on the right-hand side of Table 1, opposite the conventional role labels. Have a go at this exercise now. It may cause you to think differently about how you perceive your various roles.

Table 1 Identity labels

	Conventional role labels	More useful role labels
1		
2		
3		
4		
5		
6		
7		

Do any of the following labels appear in the table you have just completed: *questioner, analyst, innovator, compass (giving direction to others), developer, researcher, information gatherer, shepherd, nurse, grandfather, disseminator*? Some of these labels are metaphorical and highly effective in adding meaning to your roles.

Identity metaphors add meaning to your roles.

A manager thought of herself as a *lion tamer* because that is how she felt about her main role of sales training manager in an aggressively competitive business. Her team needed to unlearn some habits that were limiting performance. It was only after they realised the consequences of their usual approach to customers that they could begin to learn new consultative selling techniques – they had to be *tamed* first.

A service manager was so focused on procedures that she alienated and demotivated all her staff by constantly monitoring their timekeeping to the minute! She identified very strongly with procedures but had little identity as a people developer, enabler and strategist. All her key people eventually left to join other parts of the organisation.

A support centre manager identified with administration to such an extent that he hadn't recognised the importance of providing direction for his supervisors. Needless to say this had a negative effect on the department's performance.

Values and beliefs – *why?*

Values and beliefs determine *why* you do anything. They determine purpose and support or limit your capabilities. Values are things that are important to you, and there are two main types: means values and end values. It is important for me to exercise regularly (means value) because I value my health (end value). Your end values in a professional context will be the reasons why you do what you do – the satisfaction intrinsic to the job. If you are not getting any job satisfaction, then you will not be feeding your values and you are likely to be suffering from stress.

Values are things that are important to you.

Means values feed end values, and they are very powerful – providing you with the motivation to get things done. For example:

- I enjoy fussing with small details in student materials for my courses because (this means) *quality* will be assured.

- I demand high *quality* from myself and my team because (by this means) our department will have a *professional image*.

- It's important to maintain a *professional image* because (by this means) we will get higher and more prestigious responsibilities to *challenge* us.

- Being provided with greater *challenge* (means that) *development* opportunities will be created for me and my team.

Means values feed end values, and they are very powerful – providing you with the motivation to get things done.

Values put meaning into your life.

Ricardo Semler,[3] owner of Semco S/A, a Brazilian manufacturing company, introduced radical new business processes, reduced hierarchy to three levels and began to trust employees to take the right decisions without having to check with management. During the period of change some middle managers left the company because they couldn't identify with the new roles they were being asked to perform. After all, they had originally been employed as decision makers, problem solvers and people managers, and these roles were no longer reserved for 'managers' by the new order in Semco.

Values also change as your life situations change. If you suddenly need more money to maintain a standard of living, then this might become a higher-level value. If your relationships with loved ones become difficult, you may begin to divert your attention and energy to re-establishing harmony in the family. In most cases, job-related values will decrease in importance when there are major deficits at the more basic levels of human need such as remuneration and belonging. Beliefs support and reinforce your values – they are like the glue that holds them together. Your beliefs are generalisations about the world and how it works. They have little to do with facts. Your senses are extremely efficient at filtering out information that contradicts a belief and at allowing access to anything that supports one.

> **Beliefs support and reinforce your values – they are like the glue that holds them together.**

Here's a popular scenario to demonstrate the power of belief:

> Do you believe that there is life on other planets with the technology to visit Earth?

There are believers and disbelievers in this idea. The interesting thing to notice is that if you were to gather a dozen from each camp on a hilltop to witness a reported UFO sighting, the disbelievers would probably come up with all kinds of descriptions that support the UFO being an Earth construction or some illusion, while the believers would be more willing to explore the possibility of it really being a UFO. The beliefs held by each group influence their information processing in different ways and will support their values in some way. NLP supports the principle that whatever you believe, it's true for you.

NLP

Whatever you believe, it's true for you.

A senior manager believed his judgement was unquestionable. After all, he was paid a lot of money to make important decisions, but he struggled to motivate one of his team and no matter what he tried, performance was never satisfactory. It was after some coaching that he realised the problem with his poor performing team member was due to putting him in a job he was unsuited for – a decision for which only he was responsible. After this experience he changed his belief about his judgement and as a consequence began to involve other people more when making important decisions. When you change a belief, you change your results.

One frequent request we get from clients is to develop more confidence, and this has now become a common feature in many of our personal development courses. The critical elements involved in developing confidence are *belief* and *identity*. An example of this from the area of managing meetings can be found on the next page.

The critical elements involved in developing confidence are *belief* and *identity*.

Beliefs can change with experience. If you do well at this meeting, the experience may help to diminish any limiting belief you have about your ability to communicate effectively. Unfortunately, for many people, this experience takes a long time to gather, and some people never realise their true potential at all. Limiting beliefs create unresourceful states of mind and body. If you are lacking confidence you are not in the best 'state' to deal with the situation. Unresourceful states require energy to sustain them – energy that is best applied to the external problem, not the internal dilemma happening in your mind!

Confidence plays an important part in the acquisition of skills. When your sense of identity and your beliefs support each other in a positive way, you will be in a more confident state to learn and develop new capabilities.

> **Unresourceful states require energy to sustain them – energy that is best applied to the external problem, not the internal dilemma happening in your mind!**

I spent some time in a workshop with a friend who works as an independent consultant. The purpose of the workshop was to explore the dynamics of a number of components of personality and to analyse how they were constructed. My friend built the following profile of himself.

Identity

A combination of Mother Teresa and Christopher Columbus (a helper of great integrity and a desire for leading others to new pathways of learning and adventure).

End values

- To be recognised as a mentor to other people
- To be at the leading edge of personal development
- To improve my own capabilities
- To sustain a certain quality of life for my family.

Means values

- To analyse and understand others' problems
- To understand more about myself
- To be highly active in many networks
- To make lots of new friends
- To be honest with myself and others
- To discover new development techniques and ideas
- To maintain a respectable level of income.

Beliefs

- Everyone needs a mentor
- Mentors must invest time developing themselves
- Removing limitations is easy
- People like me because I listen to them
- There are parts of me that I don't yet understand
- All progress is made through experience and personal development.

This person is a highly capable and successful personal development consultant and executive coach. People praise his capabilities, compassion, understanding and companionship. His business is successful. His identity, values and beliefs all complement one another and his behaviour is totally congruent with his thinking.

Throughout the book you will have the opportunity to practise accessing resourceful states for various situations and trying out different values and beliefs to support and develop your identity. You may wish to modify identity labels as you progress through the book. You will also be introduced to some excellent techniques for making personal change happen a lot quicker than you may think is possible.

Exercise 1.2: Identify your values and beliefs

Here's an exercise to get you thinking about your own values and beliefs. Put down your answers as they occur. Don't concern yourself with whether a value is end or means, or whether a response is a value or belief. It is not always immediately clear.

Answer each question in turn. The purpose of question 1 is to elicit a means value. The purpose of question 2 is to elicit higher-level values that could be means or end values. If you run out of responses to this question, you have probably reached an end value. Think of at least three different answers for question 2. The purpose of question 3 is to elicit the beliefs that support your values. Think of three or four beliefs that support each set of values. If you're not sure whether something is a belief, a means value or end value, that's OK – just put down your thoughts anyway.

Get a first draft down as quickly as you can; then review what you have written and consider the potency of each value and each belief.

Q1 *What is it you value about your job that if it were taken away, your job satisfaction would decrease significantly?*

A _____

Q2 *And what does this value get for you?*

A _____

A _____

A _____

Q3 *What must you believe in order to value the items above?*

A _____

A _____

A _____

A _____

A _____

This may be the first time you have ever questioned your reason and purpose for doing what you do. My intention at this stage is to present you with a basic knowledge of how you can work with your values and beliefs to develop flexibility. I encourage you to question your values and beliefs now and again. Are they enabling you to be more flexible, capable and successful?

Question your values and beliefs now and again. Are they enabling you to be more flexible, capable and successful?

Capability – *how?*

Capability can be defined as *how you apply knowledge and behaviour to achieve a goal*. The term most commonly used to talk about capability and behaviour is *skill*. However, if you want to learn how a skill becomes a skill, take a look at capability.

Consider a manager who has been asked to lead an important negotiation for which he has a specific goal. Over time he will have learned a large number of words that make up his vocabulary, and he may have learned a specific structure or format for negotiating either from a company procedure document, a book, a film, a training course or by observing someone else. This is knowledge. The capability is in *how* the knowledge is put to use, and this *how* is dependent upon the distinctions he makes around the meeting activity. What is he noticing and paying attention to? What is the range of his behaviour when responding?

The distinctions he makes will generate his behaviour – what he says and does in response to each interaction. Does he continue listening and watching, or begin talking? Which words does he choose when it's his turn to speak? Who should he address? What should his body language be saying?

Capability is also influenced by all the levels of learning above it – identity, values and beliefs. If the manager in our example does not identify strongly with the role of negotiator, he may be ineffective. His values and beliefs will influence the goal he sets for himself. He might believe the negotiation is a lost cause or that it will be tough. His expectations and goals will be set in response to his beliefs, which will influence the value he awards the act of negotiating, as either a high-value activity or a low-value activity.

The end result of all these influences will manifest in the distinctions he will make. Coarse distinctions and fuzzy goals result from low task value, limiting beliefs and a weak role identity. Fine distinctions and clear goals result from high task value, empowering beliefs and a strong role identity.

Behaviour – *what?*

Some people learn behaviours that hinder rather than help them achieve their goals. We learn a great many of our behaviours from the significant role models around us. If you are lucky, you will have good role models around you. Poor role models generate more of what doesn't work. Consider a general manager who many describe as authoritarian and dictatorial because of the way he imposes his opinions and decisions on to others. His voice is pitched in a way that emphasises urgency and he speaks rapidly. All decisions have to be made now and there is never enough time for rational discussion. Two of his closest managers display these very same characteristics with a high degree of precision and accuracy. Have you considered the behaviours you are displaying for the people who are role modelling you?

Environment – *where? when?*

Environment is heavily influenced by all the other levels. If you have a value and belief system that supports being self-sufficient and spending lots of time by yourself, you will make decisions based on the avoidance of groups and crowds. This will influence the external situations that will be presented to you.

Managers who consider themselves, above all else, to be administrators generally have to work hard at being people managers because they often prefer to be alone in their office, checking and designing administration systems rather than interacting with people. If an office-bound administrator decided to improve their people management skills, that person would find it helpful to change to a working environment where they could interact with people more directly and more often. Your environment determines what information is available for you to take in through each of your five senses – sight, hearing, touch, smell and taste.

The five levels influence each other. If you make a change at one level, all levels below it will also change, although levels above may or may not. Making a change to your identity, for example, will effect change at the four levels below. Changing your environment may or may not bring about change at higher levels.

A high street retail chain invested heavily in a new look and feel to their stores. As a result of the refurbishment the company chiefs had hoped for an increase in sales, but following a brief increase in footfall due to the curiosity factor, there was no long-term increase in sales. They realised that the key to increased sales required not just a store facelift but also a change in the way staff worked, and in their attitude and behaviour towards customers. Unfortunately they realised this too late and the company went bust. You can refit a store in a few weeks but it takes longer to change staff behaviour, especially if you want them to perform a role they have not been recruited to perform.

Frequently I meet managers who are struggling to maintain performance levels because they have not yet identified with the roles that are key to being successful. The youngblood who thinks of himself as a problem solver and decision maker will never be a developer and coach until his thinking at the identity level changes. The seasoned manager who thinks of herself as a repository of experience about what can and can't be done in the organisation will struggle to develop creative ideas until her thinking at the level of identity changes. The corporate strategist who thinks he has to come up with all the ideas will find it difficult to get others to buy into them until his thinking at the level of identity changes.

If what you are doing isn't working, you can improve things by making changes to one or more of the five levels of learning, communication and change. Throughout this book, and particularly in Chapter 9, you will find exercises and activities to help you make the changes that will enable you to grow as a manager and as an individual.

02

From ideas to action

Have you noticed how some managers seem to have ideas which they turn into the right kind of action to get desired results, while others have plenty of ideas which rarely get to see the light of day? If you want to learn how to put ideas into action, go and shadow a chief executive for a week or so. The very nature of their job is to execute, and you will find they have a sense of urgency to get actions into their calendar. Alternatively, learn about the patterns of your own thinking and understand the process that leads from idea to action. You will find the process has five stages:

1 Engaging in a situation

2 Navigating existing experience

3 Generating ideas

4 Making decisions

5 Taking action.

So many seemingly brilliant ideas never develop to their expected potential because they get stuck somewhere between *situation* and *action*. When you look for what is responsible for ideas getting stuck, you discover a minefield of limiting beliefs, false perceptions, conflicting values and negative emotions.

"Man does not see the real world. The real world is hidden from him by the wall of imagination."

George Gurdjieff (1874–1949), Russian mystic and author

So what if you could act at work without this minefield? In this chapter you will learn more about the process of human communication and how you respond to what you see and hear from other people. The process of neutralising the minefield is in knowing a mine when you see one.

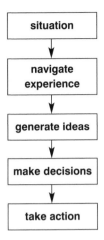

How well do you communicate?

The key determining factor of your success can be put down to the way you communicate with others and with yourself, at each stage between *situation* and *action*. Figure 2.1 (overleaf) shows an information processor connected to a communication system consisting of an encoder, a transmitter, a receiver and a decoder to add meaning to information being received. This is a simplified version of a human communication system and can be used to begin to understand where it often goes wrong.

Signals from the external territory are collected by the receiver and passed to the decoder. The decoder will only be able to decode information that conforms to the code it is programmed with – anything else it will filter out. The decoded information is then sent for processing. Processed information is sent to the encoder to be coded into signals that recipients will identify as information. The code is sent to the transmitter for output to the external territory. This, in essence, is how any communication system works, and it is subject to the universal rule of communication – GIGO (garbage in garbage out). One of the main constraints of this, or any system, is that it is only able to decode

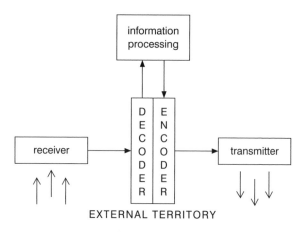

EXTERNAL TERRITORY

Figure 2.1 How communication works

signals which it has been programmed to recognise – a standard telephone is unable to transmit information contained on a sheet of paper because it is designed to recognise sound. You need an additional decoder such as a fax machine or a personal computer, scanner and modem to achieve this. This simple example is useful in helping to understand the human system of communication – our perceptual filters programme our encoders and decoders.

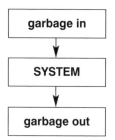

Our perceptual filters programme our encoders and decoders.

Your map of reality

If you were to consider all the information bombarding your senses at any one moment, you could identify up to two million individual pieces. Research and tests have shown that we are only able consciously to pay attention to seven bits of information plus or minus two.[1] In order to make sense of the world (the territory), you filter out a great deal of information you consider unnecessary. Can you imagine what a police officer and an architect might each notice and pay attention to as they walked down a busy city street? I doubt they would have the same experience even if they were walking together as friends. What you focus your attention on determines the information you absorb, which then gets filtered to create your own unique map of reality, and which in turn you use to represent the territory from which you initially gathered the information.

A road map is not the territory it represents.

In the same way as a food menu is not the meal, a road map is not the territory it represents. Road maps exclude road works, weather and people. A territory is always much more detailed than any map created to represent it. The map is a massively reduced and edited version of the actual territory it represents. In the same way, our personal map of reality is similarly reduced and edited through a filtering process involving beliefs, values, memories, language, time coding and motivation patterns called *metaprogrammes*. Figure 2.2 (overleaf) is a simplified version of the NLP communication model which will help you discover more about how you communicate, generate ideas, make decisions and produce behaviour.

I will explain how the model works with some practical examples and then introduce you to a powerful and highly effective NLP technique – the Swish pattern. At this stage we are still working at increasing your awareness of how you

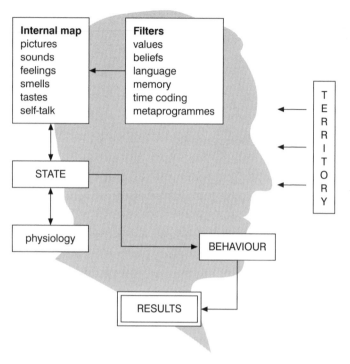

Figure 2.2 The NLP model of communication

turn your ideas into actions. Once you have this firmly in your grasp, the many techniques and exercises included in this and subsequent chapters will help you to increase your flexibility, regardless of the context.

How the NLP model of communication works

We actively and unconsciously seek out information to support the things that are important to us.

Filtered information forms an internal map in the mind by a combination of pictures, sounds, feelings, smells and tastes. Your internal map and your physiology together create a *state of being*. People sometimes say they are in a particular 'state of mind', which is misleading as the body also contributes to any state. When your mind holds on to a negative thought, your body becomes tense. This is what we generally call 'stress'. A state of relaxation can be achieved by breathing slowly and deeply and releasing muscle tension.

Internal representation systems:

V – pictures (visual)

A – sounds (auditory)

K – feelings (kinaesthetic)

O – smells (olfactory)

G – tastes (gustatory)

Your state influences your behaviour and so determines the results you get. All behaviour is therefore state dependent. This is the process which generates ideas and turns them into action. So, increasing behavioural flexibility starts with learning to control states of mind and body, and this requires an understanding of how the information filters work.

All behaviour is state dependent.

Your information filters

Values and beliefs cause you to look and listen for information to support what is important to you, and in doing so you overlook a great deal of information which could be useful. I have explained how values and beliefs can create limitations in each of the roles that make up your identity, so I shall continue this section with *language*.

Language

If you were to give exact representations of your every experience, you would bore people into an early grave. You may know some people who are like this. By our use of language we generalise, distort and delete much information from our original experience and end up giving people summaries and snippets.

> **By our use of language we generalise, distort and delete much information from our original experience.**

A common example is where a colleague returns from a meeting and you ask, 'How was the meeting?' A typical response might be: 'Oh, it was really productive; it took a while to get our minds around some of the issues but we got there eventually.' This tells you very little about the meeting. If you wanted a more accurate account, you would need to review the meeting minutes, and even this record of events is likely to include some misinterpretations as a result of words being changed or misplaced. It certainly would not contain the body language, voice tone, facial expressions and emotions which are so much a part of the meaning in communication.

Words give a very poor and oversimplified account of an original experience. Try this simple teaser as an example.

Example

Question: The signalman saw the train driver passing a red stop light, but he didn't report this – why?

Try to come up with your own answer before reading any further.

Answer 1: The red light was to warn trains going in the opposite direction.

Answer 2: The train driver was walking.

Answer 3: The signalman was watching a film of the train driver on television.

Answer 4: The red light was a road traffic light halting vehicles at a rail crossing point.

Answer 5: The signalman was observing the train driver from an aeroplane which was just taking off over the railway lines.

Language is the universal code we use to exchange information with other humans. The example above is made up specifically to make a point and demonstrate how easy it is to form incorrect perceptions by decoding words to mean something different from what the originator intended. I am sure you can relate to many examples of this happening every day where you work. In order to avoid these mistakes, in this example, you would have to ask these questions:

- *How* specifically did the signalman *see* the train driver?
- *How* exactly was the train driver *passing* the red light?
- *Which* red light, and *where* exactly was it in relation to the train driver and the signalman?

Once you realise how language acts as a filter on experience to create a unique reality for each person, you will begin to appreciate one of the major reasons for communication breakdowns in organisations.

Some politicians are extremely good at using language to their advantage. Once you realise how language acts as a filter on experience to create a unique reality for each person, you will begin to appreciate one of the major reasons for communication breakdowns in organisations. In Chapter 7, I will be introducing you to two language models – the Milton Model, and its antidote, the Meta Model. These models will arm you with the tools to uncover the deeper structure of experience and avoid the traps set by our language.

Memory

Memories help to make sense of new information by searching for a link to something which you already know. This process of searching your memory for links to your experience creates expectations for the future. A memory of an experience will contain conditions which influence your thinking and behaviour the next time you experience a similar situation: for example, a written request to a senior manager for extra resources may be rejected, and the memory you keep of this rejection will influence how you approach requesting extra resources again in the future. Experiences become generalised to the same meaning for future events of a similar nature.

Emotions are closely linked to memories. Each memory of an experience will contain contextual elements (what, who, where, etc.) plus the emotions connected with the experience. When you recall a memory with a strong emotion attached, you will feel the same feelings that were generated at the time of the original experience. NLP makes use of the link between memory, emotions and feelings by helping to exercise choice over your *state of being*. Some remembered states of being have negative emotions connected to them. These states are called *unresourceful* states because they inhibit access to many of your internal resources such as logical thought, creativity, confidence, patience, resilience, clarity and motivation.

> **Each memory of an experience will contain contextual elements (what, who, where, etc.) plus the emotions connected with it.**

A personnel manager once held a painful memory of a first meeting with a general manager whose manner she interpreted as aggressive and dismissive. This encounter led to her feeling intimidated, and whenever she was faced with attending a meeting she would recall this first experience and prepare for a similar unpleasant encounter by getting into the remembered unresourceful state. Her memory of the first experience set expectations for all subsequent meetings. Let's run this scenario through the NLP model of communication shown in Figure 2.2 using fictitious names for the two characters involved.

Example

Jane (the personnel manager) receives a telephone call from Adrian (the general manager). Adrian speaks very quickly, with a low pitch and sense of urgency in the tone (in music this latter attribute is aptly called 'attack'). On hearing Adrian's voice Jane recalls from memory the first meeting she had with Adrian where she felt intimidated – the feeling is very strongly connected in memory to this first experience, particularly to the vocal qualities. The feeling calls up beliefs that she has built around this experience which are reinforced by her internal dialogue: 'I don't know how to handle Adrian … he's out to undermine my authority … he's much more articulate and assertive than me.'

This language has a disempowering influence at the unconscious level. These beliefs support values – 'what's important here is to survive the meeting unscathed and without losing credibility'. The result of this telephone conversation with Adrian is an internal representation, or map, consisting of visuals, sounds, feelings and any smells or tastes that she may also have connected to this memory. This 'map' is how Jane represents internally the experience of the telephone call with Adrian. The map creates a state of general unresourcefulness which affects her physiology (body slumping slightly, some muscles around the shoulders, face and hands tightening).

This mind and body state of being now drives Jane's behaviour – what she does and what she says. The result of this is exactly as she anticipated and had prepared for – Adrian gets things all his own way and Jane survives unscathed to do battle another day.

If, like Jane, you hold memories attached to unresourceful emotional states, why not change the memory in some way so that future experiences turn out to be more useful for you? What's the point in re-running old patterns from your memory that get in the way of improving your operational performance? Your ability to generate creative, useful and purposeful ideas will be greatly enhanced by the control you have over your 'states of being' in response to feedback from the external territory and your own neurology. Before I introduce you to a technique to help state control, I will explain the two basic types of state which can be utilised intentionally for different purposes – *associated* and *dissociated*.

Your ability to generate creative, useful and purposeful ideas will be greatly enhanced by the control you have over your 'states of being'.

Associated state

When you recall an experience from memory, or create an imaginary experience where you are part of the visual representation, you are 'associated' to the experience. It is as if you are seeing with your own eyes and hearing with your own ears. Associated states connect you to the feelings or emotions which are linked to the memory or the created experience. Actors 'associate' with their roles to create *real* feelings rather than simulated emotional states. Whenever you want to access a particular feeling, associate with a memory of a time when you last had the feeling.

Dissociated state

When you create a picture in your mind's eye of a memory or an imaginary situation, and where you are observing yourself, you are 'dissociated' from the experience. Dissociating removes emotional content from the experience. You can use this technique when you want to revisit an unpleasant memory without re-experiencing the emotional content. The Swish technique uses a dissociated visual representation to change an unresourceful state to a resourceful one.

Exercise 2.1: The Swish technique

Step 1

Recall an interaction where you responded in a way that generates concern as you think about it now. It could be a meeting, a telephone call or a presentation – any interaction where you would like to change future responses from unresourceful to resourceful.

Step 2

Find the trigger to the unresourceful state. How do you know when to create the state for yourself? In the Jane/Adrian example, Jane's state was triggered by a picture she created in her mind as she thought of Adrian. Her state became worse as she added Adrian's voice to her internally represented picture of Adrian speaking to her on the telephone. This is an internal trigger (created entirely in the mind). At other times the trigger would come from Adrian's voice over the telephone (external trigger). If, in your example, the trigger is an internal representation, then reconstruct the visual, auditory, olfactory and gustatory elements just as they normally occur in your mind. If the trigger is external, then use all modalities to create a fully associated internal representation, i.e. as if you are re-experiencing the memory.

Step 3

Identify at least one or maybe two qualities of your image that, when intensified, change your emotional response to it and make you feel even worse (this may seem odd but it is an important step in the procedure). Brightness and size are qualities that work well for many people, but colour, contrast, location or depth may work also. Play around with this until you have identified the qualities that work best to make you feel worse. These qualities (called *submodalities*) are the 'critical submodalities'.

Step 4

Now stand up, walk around and think of something completely different for a few moments. This gets you to break out of the state you have just thought yourself into.

Step 5

Construct a new image of how you would rather be in response to this interaction. The image you create is of a different you, having the resources now to choose a better outcome. Your picture must be dissociated – that is, you are looking at yourself in the picture. Dissociated pictures create the motivation to move towards something you want. An associated picture would give you the feeling that you already had the resources, so make it dissociated.

"Dissociated pictures create the motivation to move towards something you want."

Make sure that you include all the resources you need. Resources might include assertiveness, confidence, clarity of thought, listening ability, creativity, questioning ability, calmness and patience. Choose your own resources: if you choose skills, make sure you have at least knowledge of the skill; if you need a skill which you don't have yet, then find a way of acquiring the skill as soon as possible.

Make your new image compelling; then shrink it down to the size of a small postage stamp and as you do this see the colour draining out so it becomes grey.

Step 6

Now take your original image of the negative situation and put your new shrunken image into the bottom corner. The next step requires speed. As you say to yourself 'swish' or 'swoosh', instantaneously make the large picture small and dark while making the new self-image large and bright. The small image expands to fill your entire field of internal imagery and at the same time the large image disappears to nothing.

Step 7

Repeat step 6 about five times, making sure that you 'break state' between each one. You can break your state simply by changing your breathing pattern or stretching. Speed and repetition are essential.

Step 8

To test your new 'response', all you need to do is trigger the state again by imagining a future time when you will want this different response. This is called 'future pacing'. If your trigger is external, all you have to do is imagine the event that would trigger your state. If you still get the original response, go back to Step 1 and do it again, although by the time you have 'swished' your images five or six times you will find that the new state swishes itself and the job is done.

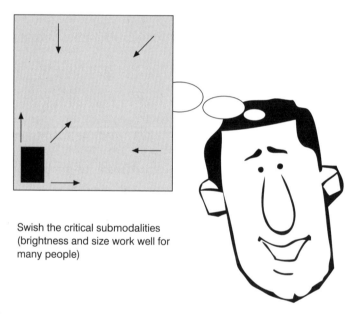

Swish the critical submodalities (brightness and size work well for many people)

Figure 2.3 The Swish

I encourage you to experiment with this technique and use it often. You can exert more choice over your internal maps of reality by programming your neurology to respond to the external territory in more resourceful ways. This way your perceptual filters are working to improve and enhance how you operate, removing self-imposed limitations.

Time

It isn't possible to manage time; what you actually do is manage yourself *in* and *through* time.

We all have our own way of thinking about time. Some people are good long-term planners; other people have difficulty thinking further ahead than the end of the week. Our ability to recall past events also varies immensely. The way in which we perceive time internally has a major influence on how we recall past events, experience the now and plan future events. NLP provides a technique called 'timeline', which helps to explain some of the behaviour we experience connected with time, and exercises to improve how you relate to and use time.

The way in which we perceive time internally has a major influence on how we recall past events, experience the now and plan future events.

Timeline uses the principle of coding time within and around the physical space your body occupies. You may have time organised as a chronological line going from the past through the present and on to the future, just like the baseline of a chart. It may go from left to right, from back to front, or it may be much more complex than this. Whatever configuration your personal timeline takes, there are some general principles which are useful in helping to understand the advantages and dis-advantages of different types of timeline.

Timelines come in many configurations. All timelines vary between 'associated' and 'dissociated' timeline states. For ease of learning I will describe the behaviour you would notice resulting from each of these two variations, although what actually happens is a switching between the two. Some people switch more often than others and the key is to take more conscious control over the switching process. The two extremes are 'in-time' (associated) and 'through-time' (dissociated). Someone with an 'in-time' preference seems to live permanently in the here and now and will often be late for appointments because the now is much more important and real than the future. Being late for meetings is a regular occurrence due to a poor sense of the passing of time, and so will frequently overrun. When attention is focused, it usually stays that way.

These people tend not to work with personal organisers, often preferring simple diary entries to record future events. Living *in-time* creates memories with high emotional content which, when recalled, are usually fully associated experiences. People who are 'in-time' generally have timeline configurations similar to those shown in Figure 2.4 (A-B; X-Y) where the body is actually 'in' the timeline.

> **Living *in-time* creates memories with high emotional content which, when recalled, are usually fully associated experiences.**

The second basic timeline configuration is *through-time* as shown in Figure 2.5. People who have their timelines configured in this way are more likely to use complex personal-organiser systems, because the past and future have as much importance as the now. These people can easily become distracted by their own thoughts of other events in the past and future, and even though they are with you in body, their mind can be elsewhere. They will usually arrive consistently on time to appointments.

Where is your timeline? Are you mostly in-time, through-time or somewhere in-between? How do you perceive or code time in relation to the physical space in and around your body? If you can determine your own timeline, then you can learn to

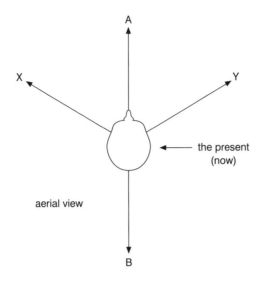

Figure 2.4 'In-time' timeline configuration

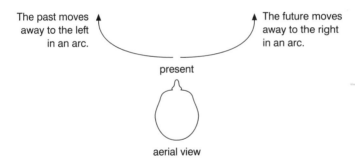

Figure 2.5 A typical 'through-time' timeline configuration

have more control over when you are 'in-time' and when you are 'through-time'.

If you can determine your own timeline, then you can learn to have more control over when you are 'in-time' and when you are 'through-time'.

To elicit your own configuration, pick a time from your distant past when you were celebrating a birthday and recall some specific experiences from the day. Now think of another birthday a few years later than that one and do the same. Now think of another birthday a few years later – and keep going until you get to your most recent birthday. Stay with each memory for a few moments, bringing to mind as many images as possible from each birthday.

Now I want you to go through this process again, and this time see if you can locate from which direction the internal images of you celebrating your birthday are coming from. Draw an imaginary line through each image and you will have your metaphorical timeline. It may not be like either of the two examples shown in Figures 2.4 and 2.5 – that's all right. Some people have very unusual configurations: for example, it is not uncommon for people to have vertical timelines, and I know some people with spirals around their body. The point is: how useful is your timeline in its present form? If it's not very useful then imagine how you would prefer it to be. How effective are you at finishing work on time? How about investing your time – do you invest it wisely? Is your general timekeeping OK? Have you the confidence to plan important projects years in advance? How about day-to-day time investment and general time discipline?

If you want to improve in any of these areas, it may be worth experimenting with alternative timelines. The one which seems most suited to western business is the 'front v-shaped through-time' timeline (as shown in Figure 2.5). You could adopt this configuration and explore the flexibility of associating with it when you want to be fully engaged and dissociating when you want to work with your diary. Later on you will have the opportunity of using your timeline to plan for a successful future event.

How your physiology impacts your results

It is important to introduce physiology at this stage because of the huge impact it has on everything you think and do. Referring to the NLP communication model (Figure 2.2), the mind and body are one system and therefore influence each other. The result of their influence on each other is a *state of being*, and this state determines your behaviour. Have you ever found yourself lacking the drive to get something done because you just don't feel like doing it? How is your state affected by what your mind is thinking and what your body is feeling? What state of mind and body do you need to be in to get something done? It is clear that certain tasks require a particular state and that the state is a combination of how the mind and body are influencing each other.

NLP

The mind and body are one system and therefore influence each other.

Congruence

Physiology includes posture, movement, expression, gesture, breathing, muscle tone, external touch and internal feelings. Try this from a standing position. Slump forward, put on a sad face, let your knees bend, drop your shoulders, slow your breathing down, let your eyelids droop, let all your muscles sag and say, 'I'm feeling on top of the world today.' How did that feel? Peculiar? Would you expect anyone to believe you?

What you did was to give your brain a signal that you were feeling tired or deflated and so the words that you said came out as incongruent to the message your body was giving. You generated a mixed message. You would not expect to deliver a brilliant corporate presentation if your body and mind were not in complete harmony with one another. It's no good standing in a confident posture if your internal dialogue is saying, 'I'm too nervous to do this – I haven't had enough experience.' You will not be at your best if you are incongruent in any way. Say your boss asks you if you want a promotion and you answer yes, but with a waver in your voice and a hunched posture – you need to find out why you have incongruent signals.

"We are never deceived; we deceive ourselves."

Johann Wolfgang von Goethe (1749–1832), German poet, dramatist and novelist

Often the unconscious will send signals of incongruence via mind or body because it has identified a problem area. Could the unconscious have concerns about the ecology of hasty decisions? Many of your 'gut feelings' are unconscious warning signals of incongruence. Pay attention to them; they are offering you feedback.

> **Many of your 'gut feelings' are unconscious warning signals of incongruence. Pay attention to them; they are offering you feedback.**

Use your body to get into a positive state

For any task there is a certain physiology that will enhance your mental and emotional state. Getting feedback from inside your body about how you feel is just as important as the feedback you get from external sources. If you are in a meeting with senior managers and you suddenly get a feeling of being cut out of the discussion – this is feedback. Where is the feeling, and how has it affected your overall state? It's time to move your body. Adjust your physiology in some way – how are you breathing? High in the chest or from the lower abdomen? Fast or slow? Breathe differently and check your state. How are you holding your body? Are your muscles tense? Are you leaning to one side? Are you rigid or slightly slumped? Make some changes and check your state again. You don't need drastic changes: small changes are usually enough to alter your state. And remember to check what's going on in your mind also. What are your perceptual filters doing? How useful is your internal dialogue at this time? What changes can you make to become fully congruent with yourself and in a positive, confident state?

Any incongruence will be noticed by others and processed by their own perceptual filters.

If you're going to make a valid contribution to the meeting you want to do it with confidence. A lack of confidence will be noticed by others and processed by their own perceptual filters; so who knows how they are going to represent you inside their own minds?

03

Creating direction

The idea behind creating direction is to harness the full potential of the workforce. This is the ultimate in getting the most out of people – creating an environment in which everyone is fully committed to achieving business objectives as a result of intrinsic motivation rather than some external carrot and stick.

"All men seek one goal; success or happiness.
The only way to achieve true success is to express yourself completely in service to society. First, have a definite, clear, practical ideal – a goal, an objective. Second, have the necessary means to achieve your ends – wisdom, money, materials and methods. Third, adjust your means to that end."
Aristotle (384–322 BC), Greek philosopher

Think of yourself as the conductor of an orchestra made up of individuals with particular talents for producing music from one or more instruments. Together, given the same music scores, the orchestra can translate complex musical notation into sounds that stir the emotions of the listener. So what does the conductor do? He provides direction in many ways. Imagine you are the trumpet player in a 50-piece orchestra. Do you think you could hear the flutes over the percussion? The music the orchestra hears is not the music the audience hears. A listener sitting in the audience front left will hear different music from a listener sitting back right.

> The music the orchestra hears is not the music the audience hears.

Now imagine you're part of the orchestra being led by an inspirational conductor whose body movements and gestures are coordinating and synchronising the different sections of the orchestra. He is not telling the musicians what notes to play but rather leading each musician through the emotional peaks and undertones of the 'story' the music is expressing. This is direction. Enthusiasts of orchestral music can often tell you the name of a conductor by listening to the music and recognising their particular style. Not all conductors direct in the same way, but without direction you lose emotional content, which is what music is all about.

> **You need to be personally 110 per cent committed to the direction yourself – with the passion of an inspirational conductor.**

As a manager you can allow your experts to follow instructions and they will always find enough work to fill their time and keep busy. The question is: 'How do you create an environment that stimulates individuals through intrinsic motivation?' First of all you must know what direction is the right one. Then you need to be personally 110 per cent committed to the direction yourself – and engage every member of your team with the passion of an inspirational conductor.

This chapter offers you techniques for creating direction, aligning yourself to the direction and creating the right state that will help you to 'make it happen'. It is easy to fall into the routine of just going to work and getting on with things, but if you want to be effective and drive real results through your teams, you need to be doing much more than this. Consistently high-achieving managers are passionate conductors of the efforts of their teams. They infect people with a sense of direction, so they know without doubt what the priorities are at any time. They also enjoy the feeling of seeing their efforts turn into tangible results that are highly valued. There are some specific NLP models and techniques to help you achieve this, and they will be introduced within the following three-stage process:

1 Getting from here to where you want to be

2 Creating your direction

3 Integrating your direction.

Getting from here to where you want to be

Creating direction implies that you desire to be somewhere other than where you are right now. There is a basic human desire that causes us to think in this way. No matter how much we are enjoying our current set of circumstances, at some point we will want change, and some people will want more change than others. It is always best to know where you're going; otherwise you could end up anywhere. While this seems like common sense, it is remarkable how many managers and their teams turn up to work each day just to maintain the daily grind, with hardly any direction other than to get as much work as possible done before the end of the day.

> It is always best to know where you're going; otherwise you could end up anywhere.

In my experience of providing training workshops to support organisational development programmes, I have been able to observe how many times the 'goalposts' move from the time of conducting the needs analysis to completing the training design. This is indicative of a management that wants to change but is unclear about the desired future state. The result of this pattern is that the future evolves as a sequence of knee-jerk reactions to current events rather than a strategic, planned succession of managed changes. *If you don't know what direction you are going in, how can you invest in the skills you will need on the way and when you get there?*

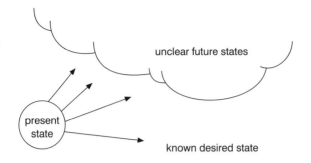

Global view

To begin to describe your desired state you need to view your team as a function of the whole. If you're a CEO, you will want to consider your executive team as part of the market in which it operates. At this stage you need to think systemically about parts and wholes. What logical larger part of the system is your span of responsibility a part? How are you going to give your team the direction it needs to continually realign behind the larger system's mission and business objectives?

What does the organisation expect of you?

To be successful at this, you want to incorporate feedback from around the organisation. First, you need to know the higher-level mission and objectives, and you will want to put some concrete reality into the generalised words used to build corporate missions. Statements like 'we aim to be number one' carry little meaning without concrete realities to back them up. Some organisations are better than others at designing mission statements, transmitting them through the entire business and translating them into operational objectives within each business unit. If you have insufficient information of a global nature to decide the direction for your part of the organisation, how are you going to motivate people and set priorities for your team?

Executive teams often know the direction in which they are going but their communication structures may block the dissemination of this important information. If this is the case then be persistent in seeking it out. What *is* expected of you?

How are you perceived by others?

In the global system, you are part of the orchestra, and this perspective limits what you hear. From your current position you are unable to judge how the audience is hearing your music until you stop playing and listen for the strength of applause or silence (your feedback). This is often the case in organisations. You can become so involved in production or service delivery that it is difficult to tell if your efforts are being channelled in the right direction. You may have to initiate specific activities to generate useful feedback from your customers, both internal and external. Unless you invest time in designing a feedback system, you may find that your feedback comes from a small number of customers and therefore does not accurately represent the majority.

> **From your current position you are unable to judge how the audience is hearing your music until you stop playing and listen for the strength of applause or silence (your feedback).**

Whether you are producing goods, delivering a service or engaging in any type of interaction with another person, your performance will be judged by different criteria from different perspectives. A line manager and a company director, for example, will perceive the work of a company accountant differently. The 'perceptual positions' technique helps you gain an insight into multiple perspectives of your own behaviour, or the way your department or company operates, by simulating the sound of the music from at least two additional perspectives other than your own.

Your autopilot is quite capable of thinking about situations from different perspectives, but you will get far superior results when this natural activity is carried out with purpose and intention. It's about the quality of your thinking.

The perceptual positions exercise below will allow you to integrate this information as you take on the perspectives of your customers. Refer to Figure 3.1. Position 1 is you. Position 2 is your customers' perspective, and there may be multiple perspectives if you have different groups of customers to provide for. Position 3 is an observer perspective, or meta position (meaning sitting over and above everything else). From this meta position you are able to observe the interaction between you and your customers. You can use position 2 for any person you interact with.

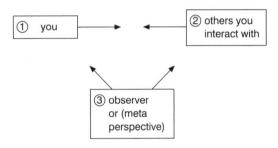

Figure 3.1 Perceptual positions

Exercise 3.1: Perceptual positions

1 Think of an interaction you have with a specific customer or with someone from an internal business unit with whom you need to cooperate. Alternatively, choose an interaction with any individual where you would simply like to have more feedback about the way you are perceived. Make sure it is a specific person.

2 Place three markers on the floor, one at each point of a triangle so that they are about six feet from one another.

Identify these points as *you*, the *other person* in the interaction and an *observer*.

3 Stand on *your* marker and look at the *other* person. Answer the question: 'How does their behaviour affect me?' Get some quality information before moving on to the next step.

4 Stand on the *other person's* marker and *become* that person by associating into their role. Look back at your marker and get a feel for what you see and what you hear. Answer the question: 'What does this behaviour do/not do for me?' Get some quality information before proceeding to the next step.

5 Stand on the *observer's* marker and look at both the other markers. Look for what is happening and what is being said. What process is taking place? What is/isn't being achieved? It is important to remain dissociated from both roles as you observe them. Is the interaction moving you and your team closer to achieving your goals? Is it helping you to achieve the higher-level mission?

6 Repeat steps 3–5 as many times as it takes for new insights to emerge. Make sure that you 'break state' between steps 3 and 5 by thinking of something totally unconnected for a few moments. You are looking for ways in which *you* can change, not how to change the other person.

This technique can also be used at a departmental or company level. As long as you are able to associate into the second position (or role) you will get some interesting new insights into others' perceptions, which may provide answers to puzzling or confusing situations and help you to create direction for your team. Here's how you could set up multiple second-position perspectives for an internal service provider (refer to Figure 3.2).

■ *Position 1*   Scope of responsibility for the department and the department's mission and objectives.

■ *Position 2(a)* An employee's perspective of your service.

■ *Position 2(b)* A business manager's perspective of your service.

■ *Position 2(c)* A board member's perspective of your service.

■ *Position 3*   An observer's perspective of each interaction.

In addition to the interactions between position 1 and multiple 2s, notice the interaction between board member, manager and employee. The dynamics between these perspectives are also important. By associating into each second-position role, you are able to get a feel for how other roles in the organisation perceive the integration of service, provided by your department, into everyday working practices.

By spatially 'marking out' each position on the floor you are 'breaking state' as you move between positions. This ensures you enter a clean, associated state, helping you to 'become' each of the second-position roles. Only by really associating into customer roles can you take on their perspectives of your operation.

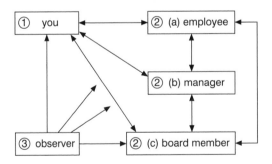

Figure 3.2 **Multiple second-position perspective**

Only by really associating into customer roles can you take on their perspectives of your operation.

You can run through this activity with your team by using role play. Some people can play customer roles while others take the meta position. You will need to keep the team associated into their roles, so it is a good idea to invite a facilitator to help orchestrate this for you.

> **Design the strategy that will guide your team to a desired future state.**

This exercise will help you to discover lots of useful ideas for improvements that are customer-focused. It will help you to 'think outside the departmental box' and to be more exacting in recognising what needs to change. It will also help you to design the strategy that will guide your team to a desired future state while avoiding the knee-jerk strategy that leads to unclear future states.

Creating your direction

Congruence

Turn your focus on to your personal mission, identity, values and beliefs. This is all about becoming a role model for your team and being engaged in activities that get results for your business unit that feed into the higher mission. If you expect the team to 'buy in' to the direction you are communicating, they will want to see that you are not only congruent in your messages, but also that everything you do and say reinforces the way you want them to go. Your team will follow if you lead with enthusiasm for what's important and with a solid belief in your team's ability to deliver.

> **Your team will follow if you lead with enthusiasm for what's important and with a solid belief in your team's ability to deliver.**

As you begin to design your direction, compare your personal sense of role, values and beliefs with those that need to be in place to support the direction. This means being tough with yourself and recognising that the way you prefer to work may not necessarily be the way to get things done in your company, and may not be the way to get the best out of every individual. For example, let's say you value structure and procedure in your work, and as a result you spend much time creating charts and lines of responsibility, setting detailed objectives and having people write procedures manuals for work processes. This may seem like you are making progress and it may be having a positive effect in places, but is your team inspired? Do they know instinctively the best decisions to make in all circumstances, regardless of stated procedure? Do they feel valued and trusted? Do you encourage them to find ways of improving their performance on their own initiative? This is not to undervalue clearly defined process, but to stand back and take a look at the balance between the minute detail of work and the bigger sense of direction, focus and passion to do a great job.

Alternatively, you could be the kind of manager who cares so much for people that you undervalue their capability by not stretching them enough, and you subdue their efforts with kindness. While a good manager will show a caring side to people, they are there to work, and if you don't see your role as setting worthy challenges that truly stretch them, they will stagnate and never achieve their potential. So what do you value about the work of your business unit? What do you believe you and your team are capable of achieving? The answers to these questions will determine your degree of effectiveness in your role.

Well-formed outcomes

Having goals and objectives is the very essence of management activity, and the effort people put into pursuing goals can produce much more than the goal itself. This is the bonus you get by stating outcomes rather than goals. Outcomes deal with the goal plus the consequences of achieving it. The difference can be explained by the following questions. Regarding objectives it is common to ask, 'What do you want to achieve?' With outcomes the question is, 'What outcomes do you want as a result of achieving this objective?' So, assuming you have described what the desired state is for your team, it is time to construct outcomes that will make the journey so much more real and exciting for people. To help you recall this simple yet extremely effective method I shall use the mnemonic PRIEST.

> *Well-formed outcomes*: **Positively stated Resourced Initiated and maintained by self Ecological to you and others Sensory-based evidence criteria Time phased**

■ *Positively stated* Take a few moments to *not* think of a green giraffe. I said to not think of a green giraffe. The mind can only represent a negative (not) by making it a positive. If you go around telling people what not to do, don't be surprised when they end up doing precisely what you wanted them to avoid doing.

This is a key factor in parenting, education and of course business. Remembering is much more conducive to learning. Desiring a positive outcome is much more conducive to success than prioritising what to avoid. The mind converts negatives to positives, so state your outcomes in the positive – what *you want to achieve* rather than what you want to avoid, otherwise you might end up with getting what you don't want. Also, by only stating what you want to avoid, you may find that individual team members begin to design their own future desired states which may not be aligned with the aims of the organisation.

> **State your outcomes in the positive.**

- *Resourced* Make sure you have, or can acquire, all the resources you need to achieve your outcomes. Resources can include physical assets like people, money and materials. They can also include knowledge and skills, but above all make sure you have inner resources such as confidence, determination, patience, focus and curiosity.

- *Initiated and maintained by self* If your outcomes rely on others too much you are asking for trouble. You are responsible for your own part of the business. No one else is going to bail you out or carry the can if you don't deliver. Ask this question of your outcomes: *Do I have sufficient authority and control in the organisation to achieve my outcomes without having to rely on other people to make things happen?* If the answer is no, rethink your outcomes and how you are going to achieve them. Your outcomes should be initiated and maintained by you so that you have the flexibility to respond to changes in the system as you begin to move towards them. If you need others to cooperate with you then use your resources to influence them accordingly.

- *Ecological* As you think through what needs to be done to achieve your outcomes, do it with sensitivity to other parts of the system. What consequences will there be as a result of you moving towards this outcome? Could there be repercussions along the way with other managers, employees, departments, customers, suppliers, family members and friends? How will they be affected? How about yourself? Are you completely congruent about what you need to do to achieve this outcome?

> **Are you completely congruent about what you need to do to achieve this outcome?**

- *Sensory-based evidence criteria* How will you know when you have achieved your outcome? What evidence criteria will you decide upon? Make it sensory-based evidence – what will you see, hear and feel that will tell you if you have achieved your outcome?

■ *Time phased* Have you time phased your outcomes? Will the time realistically allow everything to get done? When specifically do you expect to achieve your outcome? Your team will want to know these timescales; otherwise you may discover other people's priorities stealing the time you need to achieve *your* outcomes.

The concept of outcomes can be used for any activity from large projects to a phone call or meeting. Being clear on your outcomes for any activity is a useful place to begin anything.

Integration – a vital catalyst

Very often, the ingredients that determine the degree of success in achieving an outcome are nothing to do with skills, knowledge or attitude – but state.

The capabilities of any system consisting of a set of processes or instructions are subject to the mental and physical energy applied by the people working it. In the same way that teachers are behavioural examples for their pupils, managers are behavioural examples for their team. If *you* are not motivated and enthused by the direction you have set, don't expect your people to be either. I recently spent some time coaching an executive team responsible for a global brand product that was losing market share. I was surprised to find the team low in energy and lacking in confidence. When I met the chief executive I discovered the cause – he didn't connect with his team during the entire day, preferring to spend tea and coffee breaks away from the group on his mobile phone. He had not seized the opportunity that the day presented to engage and enthuse his team, but demonstrated his usual distant behaviour.

If *you* are not motivated and enthused by the direction you have set, don't expect your people to be either.

You need to make the desired future state a compelling place to direct your energy. This is an effect of the state you are in at any time during the day. If you arrive at work in a bad mood, others will be affected by it. If you come out of a meeting looking stressed and worried, your team will interpret this as something bad and they will end up in a negative state which will affect their work. It is better to overestimate the effect you have on others and make sure you are able to maintain a positive state regardless of what is going on.

Activating the future Research to discover what makes entrepreneurs successful shows that very few of them produce detailed plans. They usually have lots of ideas and perhaps some global plans, but the detail is often left to sort itself out. What is common among many successful entrepreneurs is a strategy for visualising their direction, or outcomes. In 1985 the young chairman of the Virgin Group said:

> 'I *see* Virgin *becoming* the largest entertainment group based outside the US. Getting to where we are now was quite difficult. Getting from here to a billion-pound company will be much easier. I sometimes wonder what type of company we'll be *then*.'

These words, spoken by Richard Branson, give clues to his internal strategy for success. It is clear that he had visualised getting to be a billion-pound company. His belief structure determined that he would get there. In his mind he was already doing the things that would help him to achieve this.

The visual modality is very powerful and it can be used to guide our unconscious behaviour towards our outcomes. Our mental pictures provide signposts for our behaviour, directing us to make the right decisions from day to day that move us in the direction we wish to go. It works in a similar way to a computer which has been left switched on for a number of years with the same image on the screen. Eventually the screen image gets burned into the tube so that you can actually see the image when the screen is turned off. The visualisation technique *burns in* a compelling future to your neurology.

> **Our mental pictures provide signposts for our behaviour, directing us to make the right decisions from day to day that move us in the direction we wish to go.**

Imagine what you, your team and your customers will be doing and saying when you have achieved your outcomes. Visualise this into a mental picture – make it bright and clear with lots of colour. Keep it a dissociated picture – you are looking as an observer. Enlarge it so that you can see the detail of people's faces as they express delight at your products or service. Make your picture 3-D and put in movement. Add the sounds you would expect to hear around you, and now intensify all these qualities so that the images burn into your mind.

"Your reason and your passion are the rudder and the sails of your seafaring soul. If either your sails or your rudder be broken, you can but toss and drift, or else be held at a standstill in mid-seas."

K. Gibran, *The Prophet*

When you have intensified enough, you will begin to feel success. It may be a slight flutter in the stomach area or a confident smile. Your body will begin to take on the posture of success, your head will be up, eyes up, seeing, hearing and feeling a successful future. Have you done this yet? Good, now see yourself doing this regularly to make absolutely sure that you integrate success potential into your whole neurology.

The technique you have just practised is also a *future pace*. By visualising success you have imagined what the desired state will be like. It's a bit like trying on the future to see if it fits. If it doesn't fit, you will get feedback in some way, probably as a signal of incongruence from some part of your physiology. If this happens you know what to do. Incorporate the feedback, make adjustments to your outcomes and *reactivate*.

04

Self-mastery

"He who knows others is clever; He who knows himself has discernment. He who overcomes others has force; He who overcomes himself is strong."

Tao Te Ching, book one

We all have infinitely more capability than we have ever demonstrated, and the way to bring it out is to remove the barriers in your thinking that are keeping it from emerging. As a manager there will be activities at which you excel, there may be others that you are just learning, and there may be some areas where you would rather not get involved. Regardless of how you see yourself, or how you feel about any particular activity, your results depend upon how well you perform tasks and engage your team, and so before you do anything, you need to motivate yourself to *want* to do it. Any task lacking self-motivation will have a degree of reluctance attached – and reluctance is the enemy of self-mastery and success. *Goals* that are not also *wants* are unlikely to be achieved with any degree of finesse.

> **Before you do anything, you need to motivate yourself to *want* to do it.**

> ***Goals* that are not also *wants* are unlikely to be achieved.**

The sixth strategy state

As a manager you need the flexibility to motivate yourself at any time, for any task. It's no use making a half-hearted attempt at your job because others are not motivating you. Motivation comes from within, and if you don't get used to motivating yourself, you are unlikely to have much success in management.

However you choose to engage with your work and people, you will have a strategy for doing so. By this I mean a certain way of thinking and behaving that when applied gets a particular result. In NLP this is called a *strategy* – the sequence of thoughts and behaviours that you use to perform any specific task. Figure 4.1 shows five strategies that result in poor performance and one strategy, the sixth, a motivation strategy, which comes from self-mastery.

There may be many things that prevent a manager from performing consistently well, but there are five main ways in which managers limit their full potential to perform at their best. These five ways I have called 'strategies' because they are just that – *limitation strategies*. Any task which is mentally and physically within your capability range can be accomplished to a high standard of excellence if you know how to prepare yourself and how to engage effectively. Preparation creates the optimum state for doing the task.

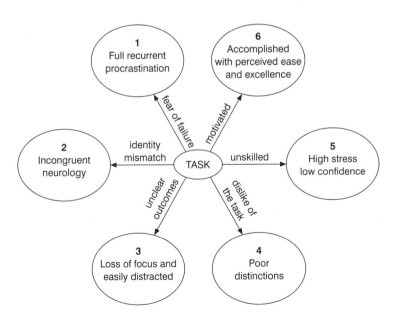

Figure 4.1 The sixth strategy

I shall begin by explaining strategies 1 and 2, and then I will show you how to deal with them before moving on to strategy 3. When you arrive at the *sixth strategy*, the strategy of self-mastery, you will know how to create a sixth strategy state for yourself any time you need it. The sixth strategy is any method you use for getting into a state of high self-motivation, and there is a choice of NLP techniques available to you, depending upon the limitation strategy you want to overcome.

Fear of failure

This is probably one of the major limitations to personal development and success. It is also one of the easiest to change, often resulting in instant and astounding results. Fear is accompanied by limiting beliefs, i.e. *if I attempt this task, I will probably fail and take a blow to my self-esteem and professional credibility.* Perception of status is also at stake here. The limitation is sometimes so strong that it can create full recurrent procrastination for particular tasks.

The energy required to generate different excuses for not doing something can lead to stress.

I know some people who plan their family holidays to avoid certain activities at work. The energy required to generate different excuses for not doing something can lead to stress. Many sales people have limiting beliefs around cold calling and selling at director level.

Thinking about situations in which you have convinced yourself that the outcome will be unpleasant burns failure into the mind, and this is what you respond to. It's incredible how you can run through scenarios in the mind and come to the conclusion that you will fail. The only real test is to try it and find out. But if you allow conjecture to decide what you are prepared to do, then you will find yourself in a very small comfort zone of what you are willing to try. Creating maps for failure and developing limitation strategies are such a waste of energy!

> **Creating maps for failure and developing limitation strategies are such a waste of energy!**

Beliefs are very closely linked to identity. In Chapter 1 you considered the labels you use to reinforce who you are. Limiting beliefs act to preserve your current identity and stop you from changing, because there is a certain comfort and security attached to who you are right now. The only way to grow and develop your role is to stretch yourself beyond what is comfortable and familiar to you.

> **Limiting beliefs act to preserve your current identity and stop you from changing.**

Identity mismatch

This strategy is saying *I am not the sort of person who does this*. It is protecting you by keeping you safely and securely locked into the thinking and behaviour that is comfortable for you. When you become involved in a task which you do not consider is your responsibility, you may generate signals of incongruence. This is simply your unconscious mind knowing that your behaviour is at odds with what you are thinking.

Quite often these signals will be caused by value conflicts. If the task you are doing has little value for you, why are you doing it? If your results depend upon you completing this task, why have you not attached a high enough value to it? You only exert energy and resources into activities that have value for you.

> **You only exert energy and resources into activities that have value for you.**

If you take a few moments to think of the various tasks that engage you at work, and then attach a commitment indicator to each one, say on a scale of 1–10, how many would you score at ten? For those which may be less than ten, why are you not fully committed to the task? To fully commit yourself to anything requires an alignment of all the levels of learning and change – identity, values, beliefs, capabilities, behaviour and environment. There is a saying that goes, 'When you commit with yourself fully, the gods go with you.'

> **When you commit with yourself fully, the gods go with you.**

You may be thinking of tasks or activities that are important to you, but where you want to be more confident and accomplished, and which you approach in a higher state of motivation. Perhaps it's a meeting with your boss or a particular client, or a presentation to the company. A major project could be coming your way, or maybe you have been asked to manage a merger for the first time. Whatever the task ahead, keep it in mind as you progress through the following exercise which invites you to design a sixth strategy state of excellence.

Exercise 4.1: Creating your sixth strategy state

For the purpose of this exercise I will assume the role of a business unit manager who has been asked to manage a major project for a new client. You could choose your own situation and follow the steps in the exercise.

'I have never before managed a project of this size and importance; in fact I have avoided large projects in the past because project management isn't something that I want to do, although I am aware that to take my department to more challenging heights in the organisation I will have to take on a large project some time.'

Depending upon the circumstances of the required change, I could use one of many NLP techniques. The technique I will use in this scenario is 'creating a new part', and I will use it to help me redefine my identity and align my belief systems to be successful at project management.

Step 1: What would it be like?

'There is a part of me that has some objection to doing *project management*, and I must first discover, from within, precisely what this objection is. What stops me from plunging enthusiastically into the role of project management? What would have to change for this objecting part of me to be comfortable with project management? I am beginning to imagine myself as a project manager and I become fully associated into the role.'

So I imagine what it will be like performing the role of a project manager as I keep my internal senses alert for signals that explain the reason for the objection.

I am beginning to feel heavy in my stomach area and to feel a frown forming on my forehead. What is it that is making me feel uncomfortable about this? In my mind's eye I see myself at the end of the project. I am in a meeting with the project board and they are discussing the problems with the project. It's all my fault; I didn't manage it in a professional way (this is my internal dialogue cutting in now). I wasn't trained to manage this level of resource and to own this level of responsibility. I failed to notice when things began to go wrong.

Step 2: Assessing the feedback

The feedback from this process tells me that I have issues around skills, responsibility, professionalism and noticing when things are going wrong. I now ask myself, 'Would it be OK to manage a large project if (i) I were trained, (ii) I could handle the increased responsibility, (iii) I would be perceived by the project board as a professional and (iv) I could remain focused on the work so that I would notice at an early stage when things were likely to go wrong?' I want a response from my objecting part here so I associate again with the role, this time adding these four resources, and check my feelings for signs of agreement.

Step 3: Construct the new part

What will I look like when I am managing a large project with all these added resources? As I am visualising this scenario in the future, I am staying alert to any signals of conflict. How does it feel now that I am becoming a professional project manager? I have read some books on project management, I have sought advice from some of our highly skilled project managers, I have booked myself on to a course to learn about managing projects and I am confident about keeping focused and projecting a professional image of myself.

I run the movie through my mind of exactly what I will be doing to ensure my success as a project manager. 'The image is intensifying now, brighter, more colour, larger, three dimensional. I can hear what I am saying to the people around me and what they are saying to me. I look and feel like a professional. I know how to be a project manager. I have a new part now that *is* a project manager. The part with the original objection no longer objects. I am a project manager!'

Step 4: Check the ecology

So far the exercise has concentrated solely on you. It is important also to consider wider implications of a change of this nature, particularly with those around you – family, friends, colleagues, the team, the organisation and customers. Check for signals of incongruence as you answer the question, 'How will this change affect these people and my relationship with them?' It may not be a good idea to become a superb project manager if by doing so it affects other areas of your life adversely. Also, if you are not fully behind the project, how will this impact the project and its stakeholders? Are you being honest with other people by taking on the role?

This process is all about creating an identity for yourself that is congruent. You still need to acquire skills, but you will be much more eager to acquire them. Having a strong sense of identity with the role from the outset will increase the desire to become a brilliant project manager. Once you have this you'll be surprised at how easily the skill will come. Confidence and identity can develop with skills training alone, but it takes much longer and often doesn't identify or deal with limiting beliefs or identity conflicts. The sixth strategy state gets you there faster and in a more resourceful state of mind and body, whether your challenge is to become a brilliant project manager or the next CEO.

Unclear outcomes

Do you ever find it difficult to concentrate on the task in hand? Perhaps at times where something is playing on your mind – either a decision to make or a situation that is begging to be resolved and you haven't thought of a solution yet? Pick any day of the week and you will probably have a number of these unresolved problems or decisions zapping around your mind.

Problems such as illnesses or financial concerns are likely to distract you from any task, although even these situations can be controlled. Some common distractions take the form of 'should I go to the transition meeting next week?' or 'who should I include in the email about the new product launch tomorrow?' or 'I wonder if Bill is waiting for my report?' when you are trying to concentrate on something else.

One cause of distraction is having *unclear outcomes*. Sometimes it's possible to get so involved in detail that you deviate from the main purpose of what you are supposed to be doing. It may be more interesting, or you may perceive it as more important than the task in hand, but if it's not tied in to your outcomes, it's not likely to get you very far.

The answer to this was covered in Chapter 3 – well-formed outcomes. If ever you find yourself putting energy into something and being unclear about the outcome – take yourself through the PRIEST list, check your outcomes and make whatever change is necessary to get back on track. Motivation likes to be directed towards a clear outcome. A lack of clarity in your outcomes isn't the only cause of distraction and lack of focus but it is a common one. Dislike of the task is another.

> **Motivation likes to be directed towards a clear outcome.**

Dislike of the task

There is no single reason why you may be either interested or uninterested in any particular task – this strategy tends to be much more deeply embedded in patterns called *metaprogrammes*. You may be able to delegate some tasks which you prefer not to do, but as you make changes to your identity and values, and as you make transitions to new roles, you will discover there are some tasks you would rather leave alone. The reason for this can be found in your metaprogramme profile. The more you attempt a task which requires a certain way of working that you rarely use, the more stressed you will become.

> There needs to be some intrinsic value in the task for you to be fully motivated.

Metaprogrammes

Metaprogrammes are deletion filters (refer to Figure 2.2, Chapter 2). They focus our attention by deleting information and creating habitual patterns of thinking and behaviour. Metaprogrammes may differ across contexts, and in business they can help to explain preferences for job types and provide insights as to why some people are able to excel at particular tasks that others struggle with. These habitual patterns are called meta-programmes because they programme our behaviour at a level of influence that is over and above (meta) everything else.

Here are ten metaprogrammes that give clues as to how people are likely to respond in a given situation. They will give you an insight to behavioural patterns, and like everything else in NLP there is no 'right' or 'wrong' pattern, just different patterns and consequences. One pattern may be responsible for poor results in one task, but the same pattern may be getting excellent results in another. They are described here as exaggerated extremes of each end of a continuum (except number 2 which has five aspects). In real life what you will find is that people have a particular mix of each one and may vary how they act and react according to their situation.

1 **Motivational direction (towards – away from)** This was a feature of the well-formed outcomes in Chapter 3 – *positively stated*. People are either motivated *towards* or *away from* something. *'Towards'* people know what they want and create their own motivation to reach their outcomes. *'Away from'* people find it difficult to agree outcomes or objectives because they are more focused on what to avoid. A *towards*

Table 4.1 Metaprogrammes

1 Motivational direction	towards – away from
2 Activity content	things – people – activities – information – places
3 Work pattern	options – procedures
4 Level of activity	proactive – reactive
5 Chunk size	global – specifics
6 Attention direction	self – others
7 Reference sort	internal – external
8 Group behaviour	task – people
9 Relationship filter	match – mismatch
10 Comparison sorts	quantitative – qualitative

person will talk about what they want. An *away from* person will talk about what they don't want. *Away from* people are suited to jobs where they can find problems, but don't ask them for solutions as they may come up with the most immediately obvious answer. Someone with a strong *away from* pattern is unlikely to be creative in their response to problems. A *towards* pattern will be seen as a go-for-it mentality, future focused and quick to get on to the next thing.

2 **Activity content (things – people – activities – information – places)** This pattern dictates what a person is likely to focus their attention on the most. It shows up often as the first point of interest when two people meet. A person with a focus on information is likely to be asking for numbers, statistics and reports, and in doing so may miss other important things such as whether people are fully engaged, or whether the location of the next conference is suitable other than the travelling

distance and room measurements. Someone with a focus on people may be an excellent motivator yet miss important information on performance and budget. Find out what your primary focus is and make sure that you are paying attention to the other areas or you may be making decisions based on insufficient experience and consideration.

3 **Work pattern (options – procedures)** These are fascinating patterns, and perhaps one of the easiest to identify through observing behaviour. Some people prefer to have a well-written procedure to follow and will attempt to create their own if one doesn't exist. However, they are most likely to create a procedure to reflect what actually happens – they are not very good at designing new procedures; you need an *options* person to do that.

Options people like to have variety and choice. They are excellent brainstormers and good all round ideas people, and they dislike being constrained by rigid procedures. They also like to keep their options open for as long as possible, so expect them to procrastinate over decisions. *Procedures* people are ideal for jobs that have strict rules and where there is little need for creative input. *Options* people prefer work that gives them plenty of variety and options.

4 **Level of activity (proactive – reactive)** Some people prefer to be proactive; others like being reactive. *Reactive* people are the firefighters. When the phone stops ringing they take a rest and wait for it to ring again. *Proactive* people, on the other hand, will use the time between calls to make improvements to the systems, and will enjoy jobs that offer scope and lots of autonomy to make their own decisions.

The types of job that suit *reactive* people are those that require a responsive service. *Proactive* people would suffer from stress in these occupations. *Proactive* people talk about what they are going to do, while *reactive* people talk about what they have done.

5 **Chunk size (global – specifics)** *Global* people like to talk about the big picture. They want to see the general view of things and are less concerned about detail. If you were to ask a *global* person about a recent film they had seen, you would get an answer something like, 'It was a good thriller – better than the last one I saw.' A *detail* person would keep your ears pinned back for some time telling you all the details of each character and each part of the story. *Detail* people tend to talk more sequentially while *global* people jump around across topics freely. *Global* people would become stressed in a job requiring lots of detailed analysis or description, and *detail* people would find it hard to cope in jobs demanding global thinking.

6 **Attention direction (self – others)** People whose attention is directed outwards towards *others* make great nurses, social workers and trainers because of their genuine concern for the well-being of others. It is as if they have antennae out, constantly picking up signals of discomfort or deviation from some desired outcome.

People with attention focused inwards, on *self*, are more concerned with how they are feeling or how they are progressing towards their outcomes. They often miss many of the signals of discomfort or deviation from other people. They look after themselves and assume that other people are capable of looking after their own needs.

7 **Reference sort (internal – external)** This is about the references used to check if things are okay. People with an *internal* reference instinctively know if they have done a good job. People with an *external* reference need someone else to tell them. Successful entrepreneurs are extremely *internally* referenced – they know when they have made a good or a bad decision. Someone who is very *externally* referenced will appreciate a management structure that gives them feedback on the standard of their work. The implications for you as a

manager are that if you are *internally* referenced, and require little feedback, it may not occur to you that some members of your team really need feedback from you. On the other hand, if you are *externally* referenced you may be giving too much feedback to your team members and they may perceive you as overeffusive. Striking a balance here is the key.

8 **Group behaviour (task – people)** This is about the focus of energy in team situations. Some people have a strong association with tasks and this will be at the forefront of their thinking regardless of any team disputes or personal indifferences. Other people are more associated with team maintenance functions and will seem to have less regard for the task in hand when there are problems within the team. *Task*-focused people perform well in jobs where they can get their heads down without having to deal with too many other people. *People*-focused people need jobs where it is important to establish and maintain good relationships, such as public relations or customer service. The key here is to utilise the strengths in the team and to be aware of your preference and the influence this has on team performance.

9 **Relationship filter (match – mismatch)** There are four main orientations which determine how people sort information from their environment to learn and understand.

   ■ *Similarity* Some people display a tendency to look for 'what's there' as opposed to 'what's missing'. There is a focus on commonality and how things fit together. There is a danger for people with a strong similarity sort to generalise very quickly and to form assumptions. They also have difficulty coping with change and prefer long-term steady employment. They may stay in the same job happily for 20–25 years and become stressed when things begin to change.

   ■ *Similarity with exceptions* This filter looks for similarity first, with a secondary emphasis on difference. During conversations you can tell when someone is using this filter by their use of comparatives such as *more, better, less, except, but, although*. People who evaluate relationships using this filter don't mind change as long as it is gradual and not too frequent. They will typically remain in the same job for 5–7 years before looking for something different.

■ *Difference* These people will look for difference in everything, changing things for change's sake. Because they are continually looking for what is different, they miss the similarities. This relates to situations, things, places, activities and people. They tend to become restless in a job after 9–18 months.

■ *Difference with exceptions* This filter focuses first on 'what's different', with a secondary emphasis on 'what's the same'. When someone is using this relationship filter, they will typically say, 'It's a refreshing change, although the hours are the same.' People using this filter will tend to stay in a job for 18–36 months.

10 **Comparison sorts (quantitative – qualitative)** Comparison sorts are filters for selecting information with which to make a decision. The information can be either quantitative or qualitative. This is simply a 'more/less than' sort or a 'better/ worse than' sort. Some managers make decisions based solely upon the amount of money to be made, or costs to be reduced, and give little regard to qualitative consequences. Others may focus so much on quality that they give insufficient consideration to the quantitative aspect of their goals.

These ten metaprogrammes are a selection of the ones you will find useful in your management role. Once you are able to identify them, you will notice the effect they have on how differently people approach their jobs. This has a significant influence on their results. You may already be applying these to explain puzzling behaviour of people you know at work, and in later chapters we will be using them to do just that. Remember that a person is so much more than any one metaprogramme – it is the overall profile or combination of patterns that you want to pay attention to.

The purpose of introducing you to metaprogrammes in this section is to give you an insight into your own thinking and behaviour. Are there some tasks that you would rather not do? Can you identify where a metaprogramme may explain this situation?

You can change a metaprogramme if you wish, although it may take a little time. You might want to adopt an opposite metaprogramme for long-term gain, or alternatively you may wish to adopt one to help you use a particular strategy for a specific short-term outcome. One way to do this is to model someone who has the metaprogramme you want, and who uses it to achieve what you also want to achieve. Notice what they pay attention to, what they ignore, how they speak, what they do and their body language – and then do the same.

Modelling

NLP is often referred to as a set of tools for 'modelling' behaviour, or discovering a person's map of reality. While I do not intend to cover modelling in its entirety here, I can provide you with some basics. Since we all adopt behaviours from our role models unconsciously, the following information will start you thinking about doing it with more purpose and intention.

For example, if you are a strong *global* person, you may find it useful on occasion to make fine distinctions within a detailed document, the sorts of distinction that you would expect from a *specifics* person. Perhaps it's a financial spreadsheet or a legal document. Who do you know who is really excellent at picking the bones out of this type of document? Find this person and model them. Ask if you can spend time with them to help you improve your attention to detail. You will be shadowing them while observing their physiology as they are performing the task. Look particularly for the following:

- **Breathing** – rhythm, speed, depth, chest or stomach area
- **Posture** – leaning forward/back, left/right, head position, shoulders
- **Voice** – pitch, tonality, resonance, speed, rhythm.

These are the main elements of physiology to model. What you are doing is being like them. You know that the mind and body are one system and that they affect each other, so by taking on a person's physiology, it will be easier to think like them.

Discover and adopt the person's value and belief system attached to detailed work, but make sure that it is ecological with the rest of your environment first. You wouldn't want to adopt the value system of a megalomaniac, for example. Select your modelling subjects with care! What do they believe about detail? What's important about it? What else is important about working with detail? As they answer, you find out when they are using a visual, auditory and kinaesthetic mode when doing the task you are modelling them for.

You don't have to rely on formal training courses to learn new things when there are so many skilled people around you to learn from. All you have to do is identify the excellent person and ask to model them!

Select your modelling subjects with care!

Unskilled

Continuing now with the sixth strategy model, another reason for not completing a task could be that you are missing the skills required. Persisting with a task, unskilled, often leads to stress and in some cases low levels of confidence.

At a very fundamental level, being an effective manager requires you to be in control of three kinds of relationship:

1 **Your relationship with the tasks you do**

2 **Your relationship with other people you want to influence**

3 **Your relationship with yourself.**

Being in control of these three types of relationship requires self-mastery, and the road to self-mastery begins with taking control of your state and being self-motivated. The more situations in which you are able to create the sixth strategy state for yourself, the easier will be your transition to effective manager.

NLP is about human communication, learning and change, and we can all learn a great deal from each other.

Achieving self-mastery

You have all the resources you need to succeed now. To explain this bold statement I will tell you about a journalist I met at a conference who had a mental block about taking her scoops to top editors. I was intrigued to discover the many hidden talents she had which helped her to achieve her current success. I asked her what her strategy was for finding a story and writing it up, to which she replied:

> 'I look for all the places where I might find information, choose the most interesting place to be, go there, get my story and write it up. I never miss an editorial deadline. Even if it's the night before the deadline, I know I will get the story in, even if I have to stay up all night writing.'

The voice tonality and physiology were congruent with the message. This is clearly a winning strategy fuelled with high octane self-motivation. It is also a visual strategy: '... I *look* for places'. So my next question was, 'What would happen if you were to use this strategy for calling top editors with your scoops? Can you see a similarly desired and conclusive result?' She realised that she was able to motivate herself and act decisively in another context. So all she needed to do was apply the same thinking strategy to the job of calling top editors. She had all the resources she needed – she just hadn't learned how to use the same resources for different contexts.

> **Strategies are made up of neurological responses to situations; they contain both mind and body patterns.**

We all have a range of strategies for doing all kinds of things. Some strategies are more useful than others. Our strategies are made up of neurological responses to situations; they contain both mind and body patterns. We have strategies that we use to motivate ourselves, which I have called *sixth strategy states*. Self-mastery requires high states of motivation. We can move strategies between contexts, so that if we are getting great results in one activity we can use the same state to improve our performance in another area.

> **Self-mastery requires high states of motivation.**

Whenever you catch yourself running an avoidance strategy, you now have the know-how to choose differently. If the task you are avoiding is something that will move you towards your outcomes, a sixth strategy state will get you there.

I will leave you to think about this, and about some of the tasks that you would prefer to accomplish with ease and excellence.

Take an inventory of the following and choose where a change might have the desired effect. It could be a belief. It could be an identity level change. It could be rooted in your metaprogramme profile. It could be a value conflict, or perhaps it is simply a skill deficit. Do you know someone who does this skill elegantly? Do you have a state of high self-motivation for another task that can be easily transferred to this task?

Use Table 4.2 below to record these and other important dimensions of self for individual tasks. You may find it interesting, and useful, to interview a model of excellence for a task you want to be better at, then record their profile on a sixth strategy table.

> "In other living creatures the ignorance of themselves is nature, but in men it is a vice."
> Boethius (480–525), Roman philosopher

Table 4.2 Sixth strategy profile table

Task description	
Outcomes	
Positively stated	
Resourced	
Initiated and maintained by self	
Ecological	
Sensory-based evidence criteria	
Time phased	
Alignment	
Identity or role description	
Values	

Beliefs	
Capabilities	
Behaviour	
Environment	
Metaprogrammes	
towards/away from	
things/people/activities/information/places	
options/procedures	
proactive/reactive	
global/specifics	
self/others	
internal/external	
task/people	
match/mismatch	
quantitative/qualitative	

Today's business environment is complex and sophisticated. Relationships in business are not as simple as they used to be. Roles and responsibilities are widening and the goalposts are often shifting daily. Even as you are reading this, someone, somewhere, perhaps in another part of the world, is planning something which will impact you in some way. You cannot really control anything. The moment you think you know what is going on, things change. The only stability you can maintain is your own state of mind. Mastering this is the real key to effectiveness. No one can predict what will happen tomorrow, but if you have control over your state of mind and body you can be prepared for just about anything, and respond positively and effectively. It's not about being Mr Happy all the time, or

Mr Optimistic, but about being able to access whatever state you want for whatever situation you find yourself in, and being motivated enough to infuse others with your positive energy. This is what being master of the self means.

05

Power to the people

The expression *to empower* is frequently used in modern management speak, but what does it actually mean? The police force are empowered to keep law and order by means of a policy and set of guidelines, or rules, governing their behaviour – what they *are* and *are not* allowed to do. The policies and guidelines refer to the decisions they are allowed to make – for example, when to use force, when to take into custody or the length of time a suspect can be detained. The government decides how much power to give to others so they can make decisions as they carry out their roles.

"The purpose of getting power is to be able to give it away."

Aneurin Bevan (1897–1960), British Labour politician

In recent years empowerment has risen to a high position on the human resource director's agenda as a result of the stripping out of layers of middle-management decision makers. Someone has to make the decisions, so it will have to rest with the people actually doing the work. But they won't be allowed to decide everything – some things are not negotiable, such as wage levels and structure, markets, headcount or investment. Looking for answers to the question 'how much empowerment?' will lead you to the problems many organisations and individual managers struggle with when they attempt to introduce it. Your own interpretation of empowerment will be determined by your values, your role and your beliefs. I invite you to think now about your own perceptions of *you, the leader*, as you discover more about the type of leader you want to become.

People power

When an individual is given the power to make decisions that previously would have been made by their manager, lots of things change. The outcome of decisions will be different because of personal interpretation, change to the manager's role and other people having to get used to someone else making decisions which affect them. Empowerment has wide-reaching consequences and is not something you introduce to your team overnight. There are skills, agreements and understandings to form first, and then, when people feel supported and confident with their new powers, it will begin to happen. Empowerment is about giving people the power to make a difference. It might be defined as:

> Giving employees responsibility and authority for decisions
> to achieve specific goals.

When you empower people, you challenge the traditional role of the manager as a decision maker/problem solver and redefine the role as an enabler/coach. It is based around the concept that problems are best solved by the people working with the problem and not by some higher order of management. This argument makes sense since the higher up the organisational tree you get, the less you will know about operational problems. Total Quality Management initiatives are based upon this concept. NLP gives you the skills to put the power where it is needed most and to do it with confidence. If more people were to use NLP skills in their jobs, companies wouldn't need to invest so much in improvement schemes and programmes. Progress and improvement would be integrated into people's jobs naturally.

The business of empowerment

Companies that empower people put fewer limitations and boundaries on structure. They nurture and reinforce learning cultures where change, skills, achievement and progress are highly valued and are at least equal to rules and procedures. They put more emphasis on contribution than status, and they reward achievement, not long service – this results from a *sincere belief* that success is achieved through people. Empowerment is an integral part of the way they do business.

The empowered individual is able to use the team for creating new solutions to problems and makes fast decisions that benefit business aims. There is richness to the working day that disempowered people do not have. They are able to use more personal expression in their role, which brings greater variety to the working day. An empowered individual thrives on flexibility – having the skills and freedom to respond in different ways to changes in the environment. Problems are treated as opportunities with no fear of owning up to mistakes. An organisation of empowered individuals is an organisation of progress, achievement and focus on creating the future.

> **An organisation of empowered individuals is an organisation of progress, achievement and focus on creating the future.**

In contrast to this, organisations that disempower people often value status and position or knowledge and expertise over actual contribution. Procedure and protocol are more important than finding innovative solutions. Working norms are protected and there are recognised ways of getting things done. Problems cause embarrassment and often get swept under the carpet only to re-emerge at a later date. The disempowered organisation values rules and correct protocol over personal expression and creative thinking.

What kind of power do you have?

Think about an engine, with the output rated in horsepower produced by petrol and air combusting in the cylinders. The engine converts the power of the combustion to movement through its transmission. Mechanics often talk about an engine's performance or behaviour. Any mechanic will tell you how important the mix of petrol and air is to the performance of the engine.

In a similar way, organisations use power to achieve performance. Very often the organisational mix of identity, values and beliefs (the fuel) is misaligned with the aspirations of employees (combustion) and makes hard work of tasks (the engine splutters), which results in poor performance (see Figure 5.1).

Power is held by individuals who are held accountable for its use. When power is misused, abused or unused, those holding

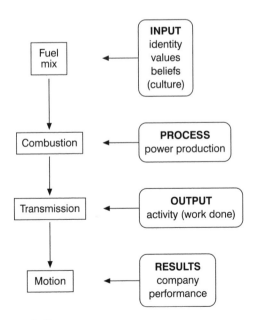

Figure 5.1 Power production

it often underestimate the importance of sharing their power or giving it away. There are many types of power produced by organisational cultures, but they all tend to emerge from one of three basic cultural orientations.

The authoritarian culture – *coercive power*

This is the traditional command and control culture, which produces coercive power. Managers like to make rules and have things done a certain way. They value position and status above achievement, and they embrace correct protocol, procedures and bureaucracy. They believe people need to be controlled; otherwise they will get away with as much as possible. Coercive power is produced by a management of mistrust, formality and authority and with respect for higher status regardless of contribution. The challenge for these managers is how to overcome the feeling of powerlessness they believe will result from giving away their power.

The technical culture – *expert power*

Managers who create this culture are wrapped up in themselves. They identify with knowledge, skill, expertise and technical information. They are technocrats and judges. They value precision, facts, accuracy, competency and right over wrong. Beliefs about people are based on intelligence, knowledge and ingenuity. Expert power is produced by knowledgeable, technical managers. The experts want to hold on to their knowledge-based power, as to give it away would leave them powerless. The challenge here again is how to overcome their belief about being left powerless.

The learning culture – *generative power*

This is the culture of empowerment. Managers identify with improvement, quality, change, fun, ingenuity, variety and the future. They are nurturers, enablers and vehicles for achievement. When people leave, it is often because they have been developed to a level at which they can only progress further in other environments. Partings are mutually agreeable and celebrated by both manager and employee.

Managers who create learning cultures value individual contributions rather than position or status and are likely to be achievement oriented.

Managers who create learning cultures value individual contributions rather than position or status and are likely to be achievement oriented. They believe that future success is dependent upon the personal expression of people. They produce generative power – a power that is able to continue generating itself without regular management intervention. Its generative power is produced by nurturing, supporting and challenging – processes that create confidence to take risks and break the norms for the good of the business. The challenge for these managers is to encourage people to stretch themselves and use 1:1 interactions not only as a personal development process, but also as a way of keeping things under control. Table 5.1 summarises the cultural orientations.

You will find that in reality few organisations fit exactly into one of these three cultures, but that they may have a mix of all three with one being the most predominant. For the remainder of this chapter I will focus on the learning culture and the dynamics that produce generative power since this culture matches the underlying principles of NLP.

Generating power

Organisations of empowered individuals share some common traits that form the culture within which people can be nurtured and developed. It is a culture with few boundaries and constraints, allowing for maximum flexibility and change. Also, by virtue of

Table 5.1 Culture and types of power production

Culture	Identity	Values	Beliefs	Power
Authoritarian	Rule maker Controller	Position Status Protocol Procedures Legitimacy	People need to be kept under control	Coercive
Technical	Technocrat Judge	Precision Facts Accuracy Competence Right/wrong	Expertise is the most important measure of people	Expert
Learning	Nurturer Achiever Enabler	Contribution Achievement Development	Future success is dependent upon personal expression and innovation	Generative

empowering people, you are removing controlling influences, and this is probably one of the biggest challenges to your security and confidence as a manager. A fundamental prerequisite for empowerment is the letting go of conventional control mechanisms.

> **A fundamental prerequisite for empowerment is the letting go of conventional control mechanisms.**

In our management workshops I refer to the continuum between control and empowerment. Trust between manager and team is the key dynamic here. Figure 5.2 shows this continuum. In order to empower people you must give up more of your control by giving away your power. For many managers this is a scary concept, but only because they haven't developed relationships with their team to ensure that adequate control is maintained. The difference here is not a change to what is controlled or how it is controlled, but who is doing the controlling.

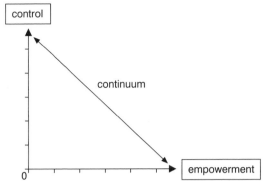

Control can be retained through frequent communication

Figure 5.2 The control–empowerment continuum

Trust develops as control is handed over. Managers are often afraid of the consequences of handing over control. It's not losing control – more trusting it to others and then developing more open methods of retaining control through frequent two-way communication, agreeing aims, outcomes and performance.

Trust develops as control is handed over.

Letting go of control then is the first step to trusting people, and trust is the main building block of empowerment. Think of trust as the axle around which all the other conditions of empowerment turn. Figure 5.3 shows this as the wheel of empowerment with one condition attached to each spoke of the wheel.

Trust is the main building block of empowerment.

Like the spokes of a wheel, each condition provides the strength to support the others – they are interdependent relationships. If you take one away, the wheel will weaken and eventually collapse. Without the spokes, the axle is an item without purpose.

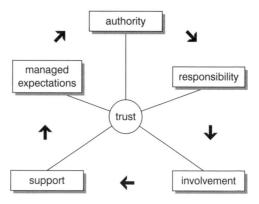

Figure 5.3 The wheel of empowerment

Power is no use without the **authority** to use it. People like to have clear guidance on the limits to authority so they can be confident when using it.

> **Power is no use without the authority to use it.**

Intelligent decisions that stem from increased levels of authority and **responsibility** will depend upon knowledge of the business, and the best way to expand this is through **involvement** in the business – exposing people to new business areas and increasing their knowledge. People will want to feel well informed when they are making decisions, taking risks and generally sticking their necks out. People will go to great lengths to succeed if they feel they are **supported**. You can help people to access the organisation's resources, open doors for them and provide emotional support for their efforts.

The final spoke completes the wheel – **managing people's expectations**. People don't change their behaviour just because you want them to. They need intrinsic rewards that create desire. Whatever expectations you set, they must be manageable. This covers both expectations you have of your team (outcomes) and what they expect to get in return for investing their energy.

Overpromising and underdelivering in both these areas can be fatal.

Case study: The finance company

Some time ago I attended an Institute of Directors' conference where the audience was being addressed by the sales and operations director of a new, upbeat finance company. During the presentation, the operations director told his story of being headhunted from a blue-chip competitor company. He emphasised the difference it made to him, how he had felt constrained by his previous company, which insisted on maintaining tight controls over what could and couldn't be changed. He explained that in this new company he felt as if the chains around him had been removed and that he was doing things he never thought he could do. He was very enthusiastic as he showed the sales growth chart, which was highly impressive. This company is now a major competitor and one of the industry leaders.

A question of respect

Everyone has their own set of values and beliefs. Groups form common values and beliefs in response to the way they are treated. Organisations, or parts of an organisation that have yet to become learning cultures and produce generative power, will have a set of values and beliefs that they have formed in response to how they have been treated in the past. If the culture has been mainly authoritarian, they may still put a value on doing as little as possible and keeping their heads down below the parapet. They may believe that they have few prospects because no one would recognise their efforts of achievement anyway. If someone did notice them, it would usually mean bad news about something trivial like procedures or working practices.

> **Groups form common values and beliefs in response to the way they are treated.**

Values and beliefs like these set like concrete over time. They create identities of disconnectedness with the organisation. When you turn up for work, you become a ducker and diver. Working within a culture like this for two or three years is long enough to generate some very unproductive behaviours that are unlikely to change overnight. A person's behaviour in a situation is the best choice available to them. People learn the best ways of surviving in situations, and as a change agent, this is something you will learn to respect. Having a healthy respect for other people's maps of the world will help you to understand why they are as they are.

NLP

A person's behaviour in a situation is the best choice available to them.

NLP

Have respect for other people's maps of the world.

WIIFM – or *what's in it for me?*

There are three basic requirements to change. A person has to:

- want to change
- be allowed to change
- know how to change.

For a person to want to change, to generate the motivation to change, there must be some reward. Intrinsic rewards of self-esteem and personal development may not be perceived as rewards if people are operating from of a world map that was designed to deal with an authoritarian culture. It may be futile to offer people a better future if their attitudes to the organisation are based on a 'moving away from' metaprogramme and avoidance strategies. And how about the second requirement? If you do all the right things, will other managers still allow people to do things differently? Or will structure, bureaucracy and protocol get in the way of change? I will leave the third requirement until later in this chapter where I will turn to the skills of the leader as an enabler and an agent of change. I will deal with motivation first, because if you can get to the point where people are self-motivated and you are creating the conditions of empowerment, you are well on the way to producing generative power. Getting to this point, however, takes time, patience and understanding – you need to pace identity, values and beliefs before you can begin to lead.

> **You need to pace identity, values and beliefs before you can begin to lead.**

Pacing and leading

If you want to take people to a new place, you first have to meet them where they are and respect their reasons for being there. *Pacing* in the business sense means being like them behaviourally in as many ways as you can without taking on the limitations that may exist for them.

For example, imagine you have taken over management of a production facility employing 250 people, 14 of whom are managers and supervisors. There is a history of poor management practice resulting in a value system of mistrust in management, dislike of trendy new 'fads' such as re-engineering and a '9 to 5' mentality. The only reason for coming to work is to earn money.

For most people this is accomplished with as little effort as possible. So, from this view you can extract that for these workers, *work **means** earning money for as little effort as possible.* This meaning is significant as you will discover after you have paced them. Let's imagine you are walking around the facility and stop to talk to one of the employees. You say to him:

> 'Hi, Bill. How's the new assembly run doing, is it behaving itself today?'

Bill replies:

> 'It's OK. I still haven't had any joy with the requisition for the new grunging unit though – still, I should know by now not to expect too much. They're not really interested in investment for production; the bosses are too busy on foreign trips finding out the latest in Japanese working methods. They'll have us all doing morning exercises next.'

Now you have two options here: you can either disagree with Bill and argue with him about how things are going to change now that you are around or you can pace his experience and get him interested in you.

> 'Well, Bill, I worked for one outfit that tried all the Japanese working methods (using Bill's words), and you are dead right about one thing. Sometimes bosses spend so much time looking outside the company (agreeing with Bill) that they miss what's really important inside (implying Bill's work is important). Let me chase that requisition for you; when exactly did you post it?'

This is pacing. It is also rapport building, which I shall cover in greater detail in Chapter 8. By pacing people's experience you are unconsciously saying to them, 'I am like you, I understand you, I have empathy with your situation, you can trust me, I have no tricks up my sleeve, you are important and your views are valid.'

When you have paced the current state sufficiently you can begin to lead to some other desired state. One of the ways of reorienting people towards a desired state is with a reframe.

Reframing

An elderly lady was complaining to her neighbour that her gas bill was too high. The neighbour interjected with an excellent reframe which changed her entire meaning around the gas bill. He said:

> 'Well, it does seem high doesn't it, especially to a pensioner with little income – but did you know that the gas company have spent millions of pounds looking for gas in the North Sea, which is very dangerous, and upon finding it they pushed a big pipe deep into the sea bed and brought it 800 miles into your house, then fixed a tap on to the end – all for free? And you can choose to use as much or as little of it as you need. In fact, you could reduce your gas bill easily by eating more raw fruit and vegetables and end up being healthier, couldn't you?'

What a powerful reframe!

Now think about the 250 employees in my earlier example. A more useful and enjoyable meaning of work might be – *work means friends, money* and *enjoyment, learning, development, challenge, achievement, contribution*. People will make their own meaning, and so don't expect everyone to form the same meaning you have in your mind. Your job is to offer people more choices of thinking about work which require more resourceful states of being that will begin to produce generative decision-making power. And your job is no longer a decision maker or problem solver, but an enabler and a coach.

The empowering leader

Staying with the example of the 250 production operatives, we can begin to define in more detail the new role of the manager, or the empowering leader, and in doing so we want also to recognise the power of beliefs.

Beliefs are like glue holding values together. The change process is going to start with melting this glue, and once this process begins you will be surprised at how quickly people respond thereafter. Beliefs are like self-fulfilling prophecies. You may have heard of the Pygmalion effect from Greek mythology. Pygmalion fell in love with Galatea, the beautiful statue he was carving. Aphrodite, goddess of love, took pity on him and rewarded his devotion by bringing her to life. Whatever you believe, it is true for you. When you look into this phenomenon there are countless examples of beliefs turning into reality, whether it's a limiting belief or positive building belief.

NLP

Whatever you believe, it is true for you.

This has two important implications. First, that people will be hanging on to their existing belief systems, which they have been reinforcing with their perceptual filters, and second, there are beliefs you will hold about these people. If you believe in them they will respond. If you do all the things you are supposed to do, but inside you are telling yourself they will not change, your beliefs will determine the outcome of your efforts – as a self-fulfilling prophecy. You must believe sincerely in what you want to achieve!

The leader as teacher

These 250 operatives need to know how to change, and you are the change agent. Once they have begun to change their beliefs and take on new values, they will need the capability to change their behaviour and activate the different responsibilities and authority you want them to manage. How you interact with people as their teacher will determine your level of success.

How you interact with people as their teacher will determine your level of success.

When you think of yourself as a teacher, think of drawing out knowledge rather than putting it in. When people arrive at their own conclusions and decisions, they are much more committed to seeing them through than anything you can prescribe for them. Coaching is the method used to 'draw out'. In your role as teacher, there are three main areas of focus.

1 **Identifying opportunities to coach**. Coaching is best done as the work opportunities present themselves. Use every advantage of a coaching opportunity which you can spot where any of the following conditions prevail:

 - An employee asks you how to do something

 - An employee asks you to do something

 - An employee asks for your advice

 - An employee says 'I can't'

 - You are asked for an opinion or decision

 - You notice someone doing a task in an ineffective or inefficient way

 - You want to broaden someone's thinking around a task

 - You are participating with employees on a team task

 - There is a problem or complaint.

2 **Agreeing outcomes with people**. Make a habit of using well-formed outcomes rather than objectives. After a while people will begin to use these as a natural process to consider

the wider consequences of their decisions and actions. Not considering consequences is a common cause of problems in business. It's worth taking time to make sure your outcomes are well formed.

3 **Matching individuals to tasks**. Take notice of metaprogrammes and match people to jobs they will get something out of. Don't put a small-chunk person in a job requiring conceptual thinking or an options person on a task requiring lots of repetition. Business is rife with people mismatched to their jobs, and in large organisations this can be overlooked, resulting in people being trained to do jobs they don't particularly enjoy. If you get the right match, you will then be able to stretch people by providing challenges for them.

The leader as coaching enabler

Coaching and enabling go inextricably together. If you are doing one well, you will by default be doing the other. Your outcome is to enable people to achieve more, for themselves and for the business. Here are two basic techniques to get you started – questioning and suggesting.

Questioning

Find out what the employee's outcome is. Check this out first if you're not absolutely sure about it (you might want to remind yourself of the well-formed conditions for outcomes by referring back to Chapter 3). Having satisfied yourself that outcomes are well formed, you can begin the questioning process.

I will not attempt to provide you with all the questions you will need for all possible coaching situations as this could fill an entire book in itself, but we can go back to our production operatives and imagine that we have identified a coaching opportunity with one of the line managers (Mary) who has come to you with a problem. Note that my outcome is formed around Mary's development as a manager, not around her outcomes for achieving her targets. I want to develop Mary's capability to make her own decisions rather than solve this one decision for her. So the sensory-based evidence criteria for my outcome is that when I ask Mary what problems she has been having, she will tell me about specific problems and how she has overcome them without my help.

MARY: 'I'm going to fall short of the target this week because I can't get the new grunger commissioned in time for tomorrow's retooling.'

MANAGER: 'Hmm. I wonder, what is your target for the week?'

MARY: 'Two hundred units.'

MANAGER: 'And what do you have to make to achieve that?'

MARY: 'Another 50 units.'

MANAGER: 'What have you tried so far?'

MARY: 'I've tried telling the plant engineers of the urgency to have the new machine commissioned, but they won't listen. I can't think of what else to do. The other grungers are running to capacity.'

MANAGER: 'What is stopping the plant engineers from listening?'

MARY: 'They're only interested in full shift work, and this job only gives them half a shift. They won't earn their full allowance on it.'

MANAGER: 'Well, this is worth thinking about for a while. Mary, can you imagine what would have to happen for you to meet your targets this week?'

MARY: 'Hmm. I've thought of everything else. The only way we're going to do it is if we get that new grunger commissioned, but I can't see the plant engineers coming over for a half shift.'

MANAGER: 'What can you see them coming over for?'

MARY: 'Well, I know it will hit our budget, but if I put in a request for maintenance on the widget sorter at the same time, I could make up a complete shift for them. The work will need to be done some time.'

MANAGER: 'That seems like a great idea to me. Let me know how it goes.'

In all these questions the manager has not given Mary a solution. Mary came up with her own solution, which may not have been the best one, but it has succeeded in getting Mary to begin making decisions of this type on her own. Success can only be truly determined when the manager gets feedback to match sensory-based evidence criteria.

Suggesting

This approach can be used where the employee is not able to come up with a solution. If you have asked all the probing questions and still there is no glimmer of an idea, then offer your suggestions, but in a way that the employee almost thinks it is their solution. Here's an example using Tom from the production facility.

TOM: 'The scrap rate is going up because we are getting contaminated raw materials.'

MANAGER: 'That's serious. What have you done about it?'

TOM: 'I can't see what I can do about it. Raw materials aren't my responsibility.'

MANAGER: 'It happened to me when I worked for ABCo, and I didn't like the way other people's quality problems were affecting my work.'

TOM: 'That's how I feel, but nobody cares.'

MANAGER: 'I wonder what would happen if someone were to write to the supplier and copy it to our purchasing people?'

TOM: 'That's not a bad idea. I would really let them know the extent of the problems we are having to deal with because of it.'

MANAGER: 'Well, it seems like the best option open to you since no one else seems to be looking at it.'

TOM: 'Hmm. You're right. I'll do it now.'

MANAGER: 'Copy me in please, Tom.'

"They say power corrupts and perhaps it does. What I know, in myself, is quite a different thing. That power corrupts the people it is exercised over."

Raymond Williams, British academic

These are just a couple of examples of how a coaching session might go. As a manager possibly the best gift you can give your people is the gift of personal development and the feeling of success.

06

Exploring your mind

Insights to the way people think

NLP

I am in charge of my mind and therefore my results!

Productive communication starts with trust and understanding. Trust is a fundamental prerequisite for creating a culture of empowered individuals, and people will reciprocate trust when they believe managers understand them and their problems. Without understanding and trust, people can be sceptical and suspicious of change. You can develop deep rapport, understanding and trust by matching your own patterns of communication more closely to the patterns of others you wish to influence.

> **People will reciprocate trust only when they believe managers understand them and their problems.**

Rapport is a fundamental requirement for productive communication. It is based on a principle well known to successful influencers – *people like people who are like them*. It's very rare that a person will buy a product, idea or suggestion from someone they dislike. This chapter provides an insight to the communication patterns you can utilise to develop deep rapport with anyone.

How people interpret what you say

Research has shown that whenever we communicate, only 7 per cent of our message is contained in the words. Thirty-eight per cent is in the tone of voice and 55 per cent is in the body language. Human communication is interpreted through these three types of expression, and it is the unconscious mind that will interpret the nonverbal expression. Your conscious mind is more likely to miss this information entirely, except where the behaviour displays strong emotions such as anger and frustration. If you were to say to one of your employees, 'I'm comfortable with you taking three months to complete this project,' but you know there is pressure on you to complete it earlier, your body and tone of voice will supply the majority of the message. In this case it will be incongruent to the words you are saying and the employee will unconsciously pick up the 93 per cent of your message which is saying, 'I am not *really* comfortable with this.'

Words = 7%

Tone of voice = 38%

Physiology = 55%

The employee could be left confused because of your incongruence, and you may find yourself with a staff shortage problem later down the line. Being able to notice the nonverbal elements of communication, including your own, is the first step in understanding the thinking process behind them.

Being able to notice the nonverbal elements of communication is the first step in understanding the thinking process behind them.

Representation systems

We represent information internally by way of pictures, sounds, feelings, smells and tastes. Think of it as representing inside our minds that which we take in through our five senses from the external territory (refer to Figure 2.2, Chapter 2). Our senses are our information input channels. As I look out of my window I notice the leaves falling from the trees and I can hear a dog barking in the distance. As my thoughts turn to the feeling of hunger in my stomach from the smell of dinner roasting in the oven, the taste of parsnips in my mouth completes the feeling that autumn has arrived, and I tell myself that summer is almost over for another year.

Did you follow the route of my sensory experience? Did you see leaves falling from the trees? Could you taste the parsnips? Whatever we take in from the external territory we represent internally by a mix of all our senses. This multisensory input influences our thought processing. Have you ever woken up in the morning after having a vivid dream that seemed real? Many people experience dreams that are so vivid they have difficulty knowing what was real and what was a dream. This is because the brain constructs real and imagined experiences in the same way. Our reality is what we represent in our mind from the external world around us and is only a perception.

Our representational systems influence our thinking, and over time we develop preferences in the way we use them. In the western world the primary representation systems are visual, auditory and kinaesthetic. The olfactory (smell) and gustatory (taste) systems are more often used as triggers to the other systems. The smell of dinner roasting triggers a feeling of hunger. In the eastern world you will find that smell and taste are more often used as primary systems than in the west, although many westerners may find this an unusual concept to understand.

The brain constructs real and imagined experiences in the same way.

Preferred representation system

People think in all three primary representation systems and most people have a preference for one over the other two. The preferred system will be the one that is the most developed and the one with which more distinctions can be made.

You will find that experts who demonstrate their skill with ease and excellence are able to make many fine distinctions in the relevant representation systems. Dancers, for example, will have a well-developed sense of feeling to help guide their movement. Artists will have a well-developed visual system and musicians a strong auditory system.

You will also find people in all kinds of disciplines with differing mixes of strengths in each system. Auditory people 'like the sound' of an idea while a visual person would 'see the potential' and a kinaesthetic person might 'have a warm feeling' about it. The systems that are not used as often as the preferred system often explain why a person experiences difficulty in acquiring certain skills. Someone with an underdeveloped auditory facility may struggle to learn a musical instrument.

Lead representation system

The lead system is the system used initially to access information. Once a thought has been accessed by the lead system, the preferred system takes over the processing. For example, if I were to ask you how your most recent meeting went, you might first access a picture you have stored of the people at the meeting, and then you might *tune in* to the discussion. In this example, the visual system was the lead to the preferred auditory system.

Some people have a kinaesthetic lead system to access stored feelings from memory in order to recreate either visual images or sounds from an experience. Other people lead with the visual system and hand over to kinaesthetic for the finer distinctions of how they felt about an experience. A master chef will have a well-developed sense of smell and taste with which to make fine distinctions about food preparation.

It is useful to recognise the differences and to be able to identify, from certain behavioural cues, how a person is thinking. The aim is not to stereotype people as auditories, visuals or kinaesthetics, although while learning we tend to do so; it is more useful to notice how someone is thinking in the moment when you want to communicate with them, and there are more than enough cues to help us do this from sensory-based language, eye movements, breathing patterns, gestures and voice qualities.

The visual system

People with a well-developed visual system think in pictures. Their memories will contain more visual detail than feelings or sounds, and they will more readily describe how people or things looked than what was said or how they were feeling at the time. Their visual distinctions will be richer and more detailed than those of an auditory or kinaesthetic person. About 35 per cent of the population has a preference for the visual representation system.

Visual language

The words people use give strong clues to their preferred system of representation. For example, a person with a well-developed visual system might say, 'I would like a *clearer view* of this project. The *picture* I have is much too *hazy* for me to make a decision.' The term for these sensory-based words is *predicates*. Here are some more examples of visual predicates you may hear people using:

'The future's sketchy.'   'That's one way of looking at it.'

'Let me picture this.'   'That's a bright idea.'

'I've seen one aspect of this.' 'It's not at all clear.'

'We can see eye to eye.'   'Let's focus on the issues.'

'That's a dim view to take.'   'It's a sight for sore eyes.'

'I see what you mean.'   'Let me reveal the plan.'

'It shows promise.'   'Let me shed some light on this.'

'Beyond a shadow of a doubt.'   'It's been well scoped out.'

About 35 per cent of the population has a preference for the visual representation system.

Visual eye movements

If you watch people's eyes as they are talking, you will notice many movements – up, down, lateral, fixed gazes and many other combinations. Research has shown that these eye movements correspond to how we are accessing or processing information. There is a direct neurological link between the eye movements and the different parts of the brain that are used for different types of thinking. When people are thinking visually their eyes will be either upward or focused on some point in space straight ahead. Right-handed people look up to the left when they are recalling past experiences and up to the right when they are constructing an image for the first time.

Some left-handed people have a reversed left/right configuration. Once an image has been constructed or recalled, it is sometimes placed more centrally for further processing. This is the forward gaze. Try this out for yourself – pose to someone the following questions and requests while you watch their eye

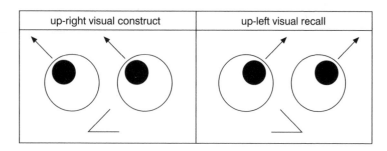

Figure 6.1 Eye-accessing cues – visual representation system

movements. Watch closely as the movements are often very quick and darting.

1 Imagine what a green monkey would look like riding on the back of a blue elephant dressed in a pink ballet costume.

What you might expect to see is a move up-left to get the pictures of the real animals, then a move up-right to construct the peculiar image of them all together.

2 What was the design of the bedroom wallpaper you had as a child?

This should get you a move up-left.

3 What was the weather like five days ago?

You should get another up-left movement.

What did you find? Don't worry if you got lots of lateral and downward movements as well; these relate to other modes of thought which I will cover shortly. When you know what all the eye movements mean, you will be able to practise reading them. If you want to develop your visual system, use these eye movements to assist your thinking.

Visual breathing, gestures and vocal qualities

Highly visual people breathe from high in the chest area, which makes it shallow and at a faster rate than the breathing of auditory and kinaesthetic breathing. When people are thinking visually, they gesture upwards with their head, arms and hands. Look at the photographs and paintings of any well-known visionary and you will find that in the majority of pictures they are gesturing upward in some way. When I recall pictures of Martin Luther King, for example, it is with his arms raised upward as if helping to recreate his 'dream'.

A highly visual person is also likely to have a posture that allows them to look up above the horizon, as this is where the richest images are created. They take care over how they are dressed because looking good is much more important than wearing comfortable clothes. Visual thinking also has some distinct vocal characteristics. A highly visual person will tend to speak quickly to keep up with all the pictures in their mind, and their voice pitch will be high.

The auditory system

People who have a preference for the auditory system are able to make more distinctions in sound than in pictures or feelings. They will often recall the precise words people used in meetings or presentations, but they may not recall so easily the colour of the room, the clothes worn by the presenter or how they felt at the time. They are also more likely to remember vocal characteristics and any background noise. Auditory people are often easily distracted by sounds around them since their perceptual filters are tuned in to listen in preference to seeing and feeling. Around 20 per cent of the population has a preference for the auditory system.

> **Around 20 per cent of the population has a preference for the auditory system.**

Auditory language

Some examples of auditory predicates in commonly used phrases are:

'I hear you.'	'Could you amplify that statement?'
'Let me tune in to this.'	'Music to my ears.'
'Sounds like a great idea.'	'He's playing the wrong tune.'
'Describe it to me.'	'I would like to comment.'
'That rings a bell.'	'I'll echo that.'
'I'm all ears.'	'That's a loud statement.'
'It's hush-hush.'	'We're in harmony over this.'
'It's loud and clear.'	'We're on the same wavelength.'
'In a manner of speaking.'	'Say it word for word.'

Auditory eye movements

When people think in sounds their eyes move laterally left or right. A lateral-left move indicates remembered sounds and a lateral-right, constructed sounds.

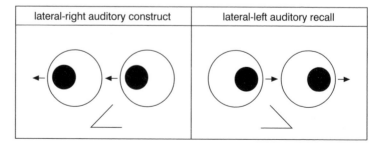

Figure 6.2 Eye-accessing cues – auditory representation system

Try out the following requests on people you know:

1 Recite a nursery rhyme.

This should cause a move laterally to the left.

2 Make up a short tune.

This should cause a move laterally to the right.

If you stimulated other movements either in addition to, or instead of, the lateral moves, it could mean that your subject used a kinaesthetic or visual lead system or was extremely weak in the auditory system. For example, a strong visual person might have seen themselves reading a nursery rhyme at some specific time in their past. When you practise with other people, be sure to give requests rather than ask questions. Invariably, if you ask someone 'can you recite a nursery rhyme?' they may answer yes or no without checking if they really can remember one the whole way through. If you give requests or commands, your subject is more inclined to search for the information and you will notice the eye movements.

Auditory breathing, gestures and vocal qualities

Auditory breathing expands the mid-chest area. The head is usually in a well-balanced position, or sometimes leaning to one side as if listening to something. Gestures may consist of touching the ears or lifting the head to listen with more intent. The voice is usually quite rich with a good tonal range and plenty of resonance, and it is often pleasant to listen to.

The kinaesthetic system

When people are thinking kinaesthetically they are accessing feelings. They prefer to 'get a feel' for something rather than hear about it or look at a picture. When assessing project timescales they are more inclined to go with a 'feeling' about the amount of time allocated than to make a decision based upon what they read from a project plan. About 45 per cent of the population uses the kinaesthetic system as their primary system.

> **About 45 per cent of the population uses the kinaesthetic system as their primary system.**

Kinaesthetic language

The following are examples of kinaesthetic predicates in commonly used phrases:

'I like the feel of that.'	'Whip up a storm.'
'Start again from scratch.'	'You can feel the pressure.'
'Bite the bullet.'	'It's based on concrete evidence.'
'Smooth out the problems.'	'It's a gut feeling.'
'I'll get in touch with you.'	'Hang in there.'
'I get your drift.'	'I can feel it in my bones.'
'Get a handle on this.'	'He's thick-skinned.'
'Let's firm up on this.'	'We've only scratched the surface.'
'Can you grasp this idea?'	'Touch base with me.'
'Dig deep and you'll find it.'	'It was a heated discussion.'
'We need to move on this one.'	'You can sense what's happening.'
'Keep your shirt on.'	

Kinaesthetic eye movements

The eye-accessing cue of a kinaesthetic thought process is down and to the right. This is where the eyes go when you want to get in touch with your feelings.

Try out the following requests/questions on people you know:

1 Imagine what it feels like to have wet clothing next to your skin.

2 How do you feel when you are really relaxed?

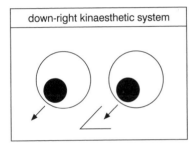

down-right kinaesthetic system

Figure 6.3 Eye-accessing cues – kinaesthetic representation system

You will find that most people use their kinaesthetic system to check how they feel about certain things. If you found that some people looked laterally or upward, it could be that they have an underdeveloped kinaesthetic system. Have you ever heard people complaining about their 'unfeeling' partners?

Kinaesthetic breathing, gestures and vocal qualities

Highly kinaesthetic people breathe deeper and much lower in the abdomen than visual and auditory people. The head is often angled down and the voice tone is deeper. Speech is slower than with auditory and visual thinking, with frequent pauses to check how they are feeling about what they are saying and what they want to say.

Internal dialogue

Talking with oneself is another way of thinking. People who have developed a preference for this type of thinking often seem distant from a conversation for long periods because they need to have internal conversations with themselves to make decisions. This is a very time-consuming decision-making process compared to the visual system, where decisions can be made as fast as you are able to flash comparative visuals through your mind's eye. The eye position that gives the cue for internal dialogue is down-left.

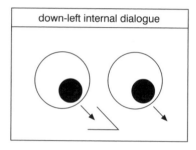

Figure 6.4 Eye-accessing cues – internal dialogue

The gesture that is normally associated with internal dialogue is known as the 'telephone position', with one hand on the side of the face, the index finger pointing towards the ear, middle finger under the nose and thumb under the chin. People who use a lot of internal dialogue usually read by repeating the written word in their own dialogue. This is a very slow and ineffective way of reading compared with a visual strategy which translates the words into pictures at a much faster pace than dialogue can ever hope to achieve. You can use your internal dialogue creatively – for example, using different voices for the characters in a novel you are reading.

When you begin to notice how people are thinking, remember – there is no right or wrong way to think. By observing and using

eye-accessing cues you can significantly improve the productivity of your communication with people you want to influence.
All you have to do is match the other person, so if they are using
their visual system when speaking to you, you use the same
system when you reply. This will be covered in more detail in
Chapter 8, 'Influence and persuasion'.

> **Remember – there is no right or wrong way to think.**

Try this exercise to discover your preferred representation
system.

Exercise 6.1: Representation system questionnaire

For each of the following questions there are three answers.
Choose the one answer that seems most natural to you. Do this
quickly, spending no more than a few seconds on each question,
by ticking either a, b or c.

1 When you first learn of a new project, do you prefer initially
   to …

   (a) see the big picture?

   (b) talk it over with yourself or others?

   (c) get a feel for how it might unfold?

2 When you come up against problems, do you prefer to …

   (a) bounce ideas around?

   (b) imagine different perspectives?

   (c) talk through the options?

3 When you celebrate successes, do you prefer to …

   (a) broadcast the news?

   (b) project a bright picture for everyone to see?

   (c) give everyone a pat on the back?

4 When negotiating, do you prefer to …

   (a) debate the options?

   (b) imagine the possibilities?

   (c) take a flexible stance?

5 At company seminars, do you prefer to …

   (a) grasp the gist of the message?

   (b) hear the message word for word?

   (c) sketch out the meaning?

6 During meetings, do you prefer to …

   (a) observe the views of others?

   (b) tune in to other people's remarks?

   (c) feel the thrust of the arguments?

7 When brainstorming, do you prefer to …

   (a) take a bird's-eye view of the situation?

   (b) thrash ideas around?

   (c) voice suggestions?

8 When travelling to work, do you prefer to …

   (a) get a feel for how your day will go?

   (b) focus on the day ahead?

   (c) look over your daily schedule?

9 When you need information, do you prefer to …

   (a) talk to an expert?

   (b) seek a specialist's view?

   (c) use the experience of others?

10 When being challenged, do you prefer to …

   (a) sound out the other person?

   (b) get a sense of the other person's standpoint?

   (c) illustrate the other person's point of view?

11 When you are interviewing for new staff, do you prefer to …

(a) examine all aspects of their potential?

(b) enquire about the comment in their CV?

(c) get a firm grasp of their experience?

12 When you are preparing to write a proposal, do you prefer to …

(a) cut a rough draft?

(b) articulate the main topics?

(c) clarify the overall picture?

Use the score sheet below to score your answers. Put a 1 in the box next to each answer you have chosen and leave the other two answer boxes blank.

SCORE SHEET						
		Column 1		**Column 2**		**Column 3**
1	a		b		c	
2	b		c		a	
3	b		a		c	
4	b		a		c	
5	c		b		a	
6	a		b		c	
7	a		c		b	
8	b		c		a	
9	b		a		c	
10	c		a		b	
11	a		b		c	
12	c		b		a	
TOTALS						

Interpreting your score

Column 1 contains visual modality answers, column 2 auditory and column 3 kinaesthetic. The column with the highest score is very likely to indicate your preferred representation system. It may help you to *tune your listening* to the right *direction* until you *get* more of a *feel* for representation system cues and *see* how you can use them to take your communication skills to new heights.

Submodalities

Imagine for a moment that you are walking barefoot along a beach. Notice the waves gently lapping around your feet, and observe the palm trees gently swaying in a warm breeze as the sound of Caribbean music in the distance has you dancing to its hypnotic rhythm.

What kind of picture have you created in your mind while reading this? Do you have a colour picture of a beach or is it black and white? Is your image still or more like a movie? In which location in your mind's eye does it appear? How large is it? Is it a bright picture or a dim one? How about the contrast?

These qualities of your internal thoughts are called *submodalities*. You were introduced to submodalities with the Swish technique in Chapter 2, where you learned that bright colourful pictures are more motivating than dull black and white ones. Now let's go back to your beach scene. Did you hear the music, and the waves lapping around your feet? Could you feel your feet sinking into the sand?

Submodalities are created in all the modalities: visual, auditory (and internal dialogue), kinaesthetic, olfactory and gustatory. There is no definitive list, only what you are able to experience subjectively. I have met people who have blue feelings and some with multicoloured sounds. I'm not going to question that – it's their world inside their head, not mine.

Submodalities have a direct link with the intensity of your experience.

Submodalities have a direct link with the intensity of your experience. One way of experimenting with your submodalities is to imagine a control panel with a sliding control knob for each analogue quality (those that can vary over a range like dark to bright), and an on/off switch for each digital quality (those that can only be in one of two states, like switching from a still image to a movie). How does it feel to have control over your own mind at this level? Many people endure the same old movies with the same old soundtracks re-run after re-run. Your internal dialogue doesn't have to take over either – you can tame that one and get rid of the old negative tape loops that seem to run whenever they feel like it.

The next time you become aware of internal dialogue that you would rather not have, move it to another location. Turn down the volume, turn it off, or change the tone or pitch and find out what happens. A common NLP cure for insomnia caused by incessant internal dialogue (this is very common among workaholics) is to move the voice to another location, reduce the volume, lower the tone and make it lethargic. Try this the nex . t t . i . . m . . e y . . o . . . u . . . h . . . a . . . v . . . . e i . . . n . . . . s . . . . . o . . . . . m . . . . .

Submodalities influence your state.

Submodalities directly influence your state. Even with all the knowledge about how to perform a task or a role, if you are not making appropriate distinctions your performance may be suffering. Using visual, auditory and kinaesthetic modes to make certain distinctions about what is happening in the business is another way of developing your flexibility.

The key to working with your own submodalities is as follows:

1 Find out what your own preferred and lead representation systems are.

Listen to the predicates you use, check how you breathe and notice your voice qualities. Ask a friend to watch your eye movements. You could set up your own test with the help of a friend.

2 Be aware of your own behaviour and recognise from the feedback you get where you need to make changes.

Where would you like to have better choices and improve the results you get?

3 Notice from your own cues what representation systems you are using to produce the behaviour.

Be fully aware of how your state changes as you begin to think about these situations. Which system leads you into the preferred system you use in each of these situations?

4 Use your control panel to change your submodalities or to change representation systems completely.

Start by making any change. If one change doesn't work, try another, and another.

Here's a list of some of the more common submodalities in each of the three main representation systems.

Visual submodalities

- Associated or dissociated
- Colour or black and white
- Location
- Size
- Size of yourself (in the picture) in relation to the overall image
- Contrast
- Framed or panoramic

- Brightness
- Depth (two- or three-dimensional)
- Focus
- Transparent or opaque
- Orientation (tilt, angle)
- The number of different images
- Moving or still
- Speed of movement
- Magnification of separate objects

Auditory submodalities

- Volume
- Location of sounds
- Words or other sounds or both
- Stereo or mono
- Tone
- Duration
- Clarity
- Pitch
- Resonance

Kinaesthetic submodalities

- Pressure
- Location
- Weight
- Local or whole body sensation
- Shape
- Texture
- Temperature
- Intensity

Everything begins with a thought, and how you manifest your thoughts with internal images, sounds and dialogue has an impact on the decisions you make. Having an effective thought process is a much valued attribute in business, but when you consider the many variations and differences possible between individuals, is it any wonder why communication often fails to have the intended effect? But when you have learned how to modify your own communication process you can begin to communicate in ways which convey the meaning you truly intend to get across, and do it with increasing elegance.

"Half our mistakes in life arise from feeling where we ought to think, and thinking where we ought to feel."

J. Churton Collins (1848–1908), English author, critic and scholar

The more you tune in to others' communication preferences the more you will be understood, and the more impact you will have. One of the most basic needs we have as human beings is the need to be understood. When you are able to convey understanding to people they will trust you more, and as a consequence your sphere of influence within the group or organisation will grow.

07

The power of words

Language is our universal system for communicating meaning, understanding and experience to others and ourselves. Even though words account for only 7 per cent of meaning, they can pack tremendous power into our communication. In eastern wisdom words are often referred to as arrows that, once they have left the bow, will strike their target with great impact.

"The stroke of the whip maketh marks in the flesh: but the stroke of the tongue breaketh the bones. Many have fallen by the edge of the sword: but not so many as have fallen by the tongue."
Apocrypha, Ecclesiasticus

You may have experienced the negative effects of words which are spoken with seemingly no concern for the receiver's experience, values or feelings. All communication has a power rating, and this chapter contains many ways in which you can increase the rating of your communication to ecologically accomplish your outcomes.

All communication has a power rating.

Language is a tool that can be used positively to apply leverage in situations and help you move towards your goals. It is a diagnostic tool and a tool of influence and persuasion. It provides clues to the thinking patterns and processes of others, and the way you use it can either constrain or enhance your flexibility. There are people who have become skilled in the art of discussion and debate, who enjoy the act of talking with no particular end in mind other than to put forward an opinion, argument or proposition, or merely to fill space with words.

Intention, purpose and outcome

Language is one of the perceptual filters that generalise, distort and delete sensory information to form your unique version of reality. Language conforms to a specific structure and a set of rules sequencing words so that you can be understood by others. These rules are so deeply embedded into your unconscious that thought and speech are synthesised into one process.

> **Thought and speech are synthesised into one process.**

Whenever we open our mouths, words might come out, and once they're out it's too late to change them – like arrows leaving the bow. If only it were possible to backtrack and choose our words more wisely, we could significantly improve our communication skill. Words have an instant effect on the people listening. An engineering manager I used to know would hijack any meeting by talking almost nonstop and digressing from the business in hand. As a result other people at his meetings would 'tune-out' when he was talking.

> **All communication has an intention behind it.**

How true is your language to your experience?

The NLP model of communication in Chapter 2 explained how language filters your experience. If I were to tell you about a recent trip I made to Germany, filling in every moment of my experience – the size, shape, colour of the hotel, the type of windows it had, all my conversations with waiters, the weather each day, etc. – you would become bored very quickly. So I select what I consider the highlights and leave out the rest.

Words can never be the original experience they seek to represent – they are too far removed from it. First we have an experience, which we represent with our internal representation systems, and when we want to talk to others about the experience, we recall the sensory information from memory and communicate it to others in words. The words we use are not the event they represent. Our memories contain judgements, opinions and perceptions we have applied to our original experience.

NLP

The words we use are not the event they represent.

Let's take a look at some ways to upgrade the power rating of your communication.

What's your chunk size?

Communication takes place on different levels. See how many different levels you can detect in this conversation among a group of accountants.

JIM: 'Year-end results look promising.'

KEN: 'They would look even better if we could cut our stationery costs.'

SARAH: 'Never mind stationery costs, do you know what we get charged for international calls routed to mobiles?'

KIM: 'The phone companies are making huge profits on international business these days.'

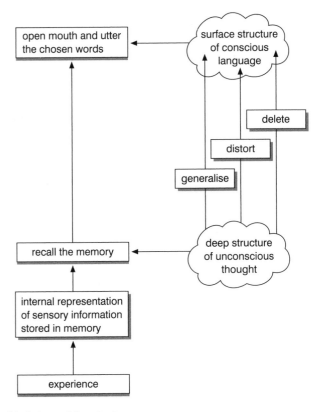

Figure 7.1 Surface and deep structure

In this example some of the accountants are referring to details (three-minute phone call and stationery costs) and others to much bigger concepts (year-end results, phone companies' profits). If we were to talk about transport, *the transport system* is a large chunk (global) and *the bus that takes me to work* is a small chunk (specific). You may recall from Chapter 4 a metaprogramme based on this concept.

If you were to draw a chart of the changing levels, it might look like this:

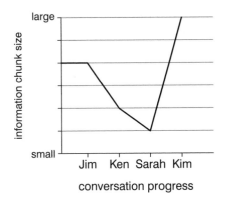

Some people prefer to speak globally, while others like to be specific. Flexible communication requires the ability to chunk up, down or laterally depending upon the situation. Just staying at one level is certainly inflexible. Effective politicians are experts at this. If you were to ask a politician a relatively small-chunk question like 'what are you going to do about income tax?', a skilled politician will chunk upward, i.e. 'income tax is but one element in the fight to keep inflation under control which we have said will remain at the top of our agenda.'

This response chunked up from *income tax* to *inflation*. A lateral move remains at the same chunk size. Figure 7.2 demonstrates all three moves – up, down and lateral – with the question that triggers the move in each direction.

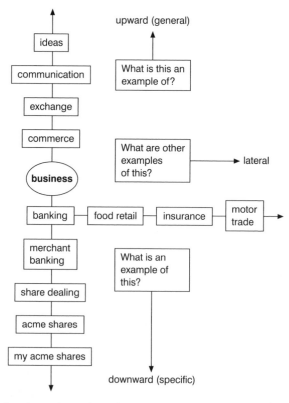

Figure 7.2 **Stepping up, down and laterally**

You will find that some people have the flexibility to move around and relate to people using a mix of chunk sizes. Other people seem to get stuck in either big picture or detail. People who are stuck in detail have a lot to say, and some seem to have no mechanism for stopping. Their conversations may seem cluttered and tedious. People who get stuck in big picture tend to have shorter conversations as they don't feel the need to explain and describe things fully. What they do well is generalise. As a manager you want to have the flexibility to move up, down and across this model depending upon what the situation calls for. Most importantly, as your career progresses and you become more involved in business strategies, you will need the ability to think and speak in big chunks. Managers who are stuck in detail tend to micro-manage their staff as they find it hard to let go of the details.

If you are addressing a large group of people, it is often best to keep your information to a large-chunk size and avoid specifics. This allows people to put their own meaning to your words, and you will avoid getting tied up with details and technicalities. Chunking up will help you to create direction for your team by defining global objectives for the business. Once you have described these, it's just a matter of chunking down until you reach the level at which your part of the organisation operates.

Be aware of your own preference for chunk size, and notice the preferences of other people. Developing your ability to move up, down and across will increase the flexibility of your communication.

Artfully vague language – the Milton Model

If you chunk up and stay there, your conversations will be 'artfully vague'. This is the language of presidents, politicians, professional orators, hypnotherapists and CEOs. It is the language that Hitler, Martin Luther King and Gandhi all used to pursue their very different aims. Artfully vague language is a powerful language when used with intention. It is powerful because it uses words that have no specific meaning and which anyone can believe. It uses gross generalisations, deletions and distortions that give a general message while allowing individuals to apply their own specific meaning.

Company mission statements are built from artfully vague language so that they can have meaning for the whole organisation. If mission statements were specific, they would be so lengthy no one would take any notice of them. Consider this mission statement – 'we aim to be number one'. It doesn't say very much at all, but its meaning can permeate through the organisation, being interpreted by each person in their own way. Artfully vague language is known as the Milton Model[1] in NLP after the late Milton Erickson, who was recognised around the world for being a highly effective and unconventional hypnotherapist.

The Meta Model

The Meta Model is the antidote to artfully vague language. Clearly there will be many times where specificity is required, such as a group problem-solving session where measurement is an important criterion. The Meta Model provides the tests to recover information which has been generalised, distorted and deleted by our perceptual filters. It is known as the *precision tool* and is often likened to a surgeon's scalpel, cutting in precisely the right place and dissecting to remove diseased tissue.

There will be times when you will want to be artfully vague – speaking at a large convention or sending a note of commendation to a company division, for example. There will be other times when you will want to use the Meta Model to get agreement on an important detail with someone who is generalising. I will run through each of the Milton Model language patterns and give the Meta Model test with an example for each one. The examples given are not intended to demonstrate what to say in any particular context, but to show you various artfully vague patterns and the Meta Model responses that suggest what is missing. The specific responses given here are not intended to be used as shown, as to do so will probably blow any rapport you have managed to create. It is up to you to decide how to bring the focus on to the missing information, depending upon your situation and your outcome. I suggest you couch your question or statement in such a way that it causes no offence, and can be taken as an intelligent and curious remark. In this way you are more likely to have a positive influence on the other person. Simply to use the examples as given here may alienate the other person.

Nominalisations

Take the word *flexibility*, which should be a familiar word to you by now, and ask ten people from your organisation what it means to them. I guarantee you will get ten different answers (and some may well surprise you). The word *flexibility* belongs to a category of words called 'nominalisations', which are process words that have been changed into nouns, i.e. to 'flex' (process) and the state of 'flexibility' (noun). Using words like this allows people to add their own meaning, from their own model of the world. Here's a nominalised speech:

> 'I have a great *admiration* and *respect* for the Southern team whose *delivery* of our new system has set new standards of *performance* and redefined what *success* means to our company.' (The words in italics are nominalisations.)

Now here are the Meta Model responses to this which result from changing the noun back into a process:

■ How do you admire them?

■ How do you show your respect?

■ How did they deliver and to whom did they deliver?

■ How exactly did they perform?

■ What did they succeed at?

Unspecified nouns

This pattern deletes specific 'who' and 'what' information as in the following examples:

■ 'They will have it ready by next Tuesday.'

■ 'The entire project was chaotic from beginning to end.'

■ 'Managers should lead from the front.'

■ 'Accountants shouldn't be trusted with these matters.'

And the Meta Model responses:

■ Who will have it ready?

■ Which project? What was chaotic about it?

■ Which managers? Who or what should they lead? Whose front?

■ Which accountants shouldn't be trusted? What matters?

Unspecified verbs

This is simply a deletion of the 'how' information. For example:

■ 'We launched the product.'

■ 'The order was finally completed.'

■ 'We are doing our best.'

■ 'We are taking an aggressive approach in this marketplace.'

And the Meta Model responses:

■ How specifically did you launch the product?

- How specifically was the order completed?
- How precisely are you doing your best?
- How explicitly are you taking an aggressive approach?

Lost performative

These are value judgements and you can notice them in just about every sentence uttered by a politician. Examples are: 'It's absolutely clear that we got this policy right'; 'The future of this industry is secure'; 'We have the best health system in the western world.' These statements are all judgements that can have an enormous impact when used in a high-level address or presentation. If you consider any dispute where the parties involved have different values, you will hear an abundance of lost performatives.

Here are some more examples:

- 'We have the best IT system on the market today.'
- 'Our service is falling behind our competitors.'
- 'It's obvious that what we need to do is diversify.'
- 'She's clearly out in front of the rest.'

And the Meta Model responses:

- According to whom?
- Who says so?
- It's obvious to whom?
- To whom is it clear she is out in front?

Comparisons

One of our human traits is the ability to make comparisons. We continually look around us for similarities or differences. This is a fundamental part of our brain's processing function. Yet often, in conversation, part of the information we use for comparison gets left out. Here are some examples:

- 'It's better to take this approach.'
- 'You'll find the sales are increasing significantly.'
- 'We're the best team for the job.'
- 'She's an ideal candidate.'

And the Meta Model responses:

- Better compared with what?
- Increasing compared against what?
- Best with respect to what?
- Ideal compared with whom?

Mind reading

This pattern is about assuming you know what another person is thinking. Let's suppose you are in a meeting and, as you follow the line of discussion, you become concerned that a project you were managing is coming under close scrutiny and some criticism. You may begin to have thoughts about the relationship between you and the critics – perhaps one of them appears to be attacking more than the others. It could be the tone of voice or the body language that you are responding to, and suddenly you find yourself thinking 'he's got it in for me'.

This is a classic mind read. How do you know he has it in for you? It would be more useful to notice both the verbal and nonverbal cues without attaching meaning. For example:

> He's leaning forward, and his voice has a sharp edge to it compared to how he usually speaks. He is talking about the problems we had in stage two of the project.

Assuming anything further than this is tempting fate. If your project is being torn into, you will need your mind's processing power for rational analysis of the situation, so better not to waste it on mind reading. Even worse, while you are mind reading you are deleting lots of other information that could be useful to you.

Here is another example:

> I know that you are all wondering who the special guest is going to be and, like me, you won't want to miss the important announcement which you have all been waiting for.

And the Meta Model responses:

- How do you know we are all wondering?
- How do you know I won't want to miss the announcement?
- How do you know we have been waiting for the announcement?

Cause and effect

This pattern involves one thing having a causal relationship to another – A causes B. The problem sometimes created with this pattern is the construction of cause/effects that act as limitations.

For example, compare 'the sun makes the flowers grow' with 'the CEO makes me nervous'. The former is a biological act of nature where the sun contributes to the process of photosynthesis having a direct biological effect on the flowers. In the latter case, it is not the CEO that causes nervousness – there is no direct biological link. Flowers cannot *choose* to photosynthesise, but you can *choose* your 'state' of mind in response to the way you interpret the world.

Using the Meta Model on your internal dialogue will help you to retain control of your state. The Meta Model challenge to the previous example would be, 'How exactly does the CEO make you nervous?' Or you could say, 'How do you manage to make yourself nervous when you're with the CEO?'

Here are some more examples:

- 'If I took a holiday the work would suffer.'
- 'Meetings make me tired.'
- 'Involving the workforce will make many improvements.'

And the Meta Model responses:

- How would your taking a holiday cause the work to suffer?
- How do you manage to make yourself tired when you're at meetings?
- How will involvement lead to improvements?

Complex equivalence

This pattern involves two statements that are given the same meaning. For example, 'Your being here means we can start to make progress.' *Making progress* is attributed to *your being here*. Here are some more examples:

- 'Arriving late means you have no respect for me.'
- 'I can tell you're angry by your tapping foot.'
- 'These results mean we can relax for a while.'
- 'Being in the top team means we can be proud of ourselves.'

And the Meta Model responses:

- How does being late mean I have no respect for you?
- How have you come to the conclusion that my tapping foot means I am angry?
- How do the results mean that we can relax?
- How does being in the top team mean we can be proud?

Presupposition

These are the assumptions we use from day to day that must be true for our language to make sense. For example, 'we'll pull out *all* the stops on this campaign' presupposes that on other campaigns not *all* of the stops were pulled out. Here are some more examples:

- 'Are you using Acme Ltd to market the new product?'
  (Presupposes I am going to market a new product.)
- 'When you have my experience you'll understand my decision.'
  (Presupposes I don't have your experience and I don't understand your decision.)
- 'Are you going to pilot the project in the north or the south?'
  (Presupposes I am going to pilot the project.)
- 'You have made the same mistake as everyone else.'
  (Presupposes everyone else has made this mistake.)

And the Meta Model responses:

- What makes you think I have decided to market the product?
- What makes you think I don't have your experience?
- How do you know I don't understand your decision?
- What leads you to believe I am going to pilot this project?
- How do you know everyone else has made this mistake?

Universal quantifiers

These are patterns of generalisation and include words like *all, never, every, none, everyone* and *always*. Take 'all politicians are untrustworthy'. This statement applies a belief about politics to all possible political activities.

Generalising is a way of taking a statement that was probably used to describe one experience and applying it to cover all possibilities. Often these statements are opinions or beliefs, and when we apply these to all possibilities there is a high risk of creating limitations to our thinking process and therefore limiting our flexibility. Here are some examples:

- 'We must all increase our productivity.'

- 'Sales have taken a fall this year.'

- 'Managers don't understand us.'

- 'I can't get people to cooperate with me.'

- 'Property is too expensive in this area.'

And the Meta Model responses:

- *All*?

- Have *all* sales taken a fall?

- Has *one* manager ever understood you?

- Isn't there *one* person who will cooperate?

- *All* property?

Generalisations

In addition to the universal quantifiers there are a host of other generalisations. Many words used in business are just generalisations of an idea or concept. Ask people what *quality* means and they will probably come up with statements they have learned like 'getting it right first time' or 'signing your work with excellence'.

Generalisations are useful for global communication. However, the corporate speak of mission statements and strategy must, at some stage, be translated into language that people can relate to and help them make smart decisions that move the business forward. Otherwise mission statements will remain just empty, useless words.

Modal operators of necessity

From early childhood we are conditioned to conform to rules. I remember from my own first months at infant school being told where I *must* and *mustn't* go; where I *ought* to be at certain times; what I *had* to say when addressing teachers; what I *should* and *shouldn't* do when in the playground. And this conditioning stays with us throughout our lives. We create order in our environment by imposing rules and procedures on ourselves and others. Sometimes the language we choose to build our rule structures and moral code restricts our flexibility.

The modal operators you choose have an influence on your motivation. Someone who thinks 'I must complete the order today' is more likely to get the job done than a person who thinks 'I might get this order completed today'.

If you are finding it difficult to motivate yourself to do something, check out the modal operators you are using. A shift from *might* through *must* to *will* can make a big difference, especially when you also use the submodalities of *will* from some other task in which you are highly motivated. Use this with the sixth strategy state (Chapter 4) to add even more power to your state of motivation.

Modal operators of necessity usually contain the words *ought/ ought not, should/shouldn't, must/mustn't*, i.e. 'I mustn't be late finishing this report.' The Meta Model response to a modal operator of necessity is simply, 'What would happen if you (did/ didn't)/(were/were not)?'

Modal operator of possibility

These patterns determine the boundaries of what is possible and impossible for you. In Chapter 1, the first two responses to the square peg in the round hole problem contained modal operators of possibility – 'I *can't* do that' and 'Yes I *can* do that'.

You probably set a great many limitations for yourself with these simple words. I'm not suggesting you can do anything you wish – some things are physically impossible because of the laws of nature, such as walking on water. However, much potential remains suppressed because of limiting beliefs, and you can notice these through language and the choice of modal operators.

Any time you find yourself using the word *can't,* ask yourself if it is a physical limitation or whether the words *won't* or *haven't learned yet* are more appropriate. As I mentioned in Chapter 1, *can't* is a disempowering word, except where it is used to negate a limitation such as 'you can't not succeed'. Here are some examples of this pattern:

- 'I can't manage this workload.'
- 'We mustn't upset the applecart.'
- 'It's impossible to get through to him.'
- 'They can't see my argument at all.'

And the Meta Model responses:

- What prevents you from managing it?
- What could happen if you did upset it?
- What stops you from getting through?
- What prevents them from seeing it?

Milton Model language contains many more subtleties than I have so far mentioned in this chapter. Developing rapport, pacing and leading, influencing and offering more behavioural choices are ways of using it, and in the following two chapters I will introduce you to some practical applications.

To end this section on the Milton Model and Meta Model, here's a short extract of Gordon Brown's keynote speech to the Fabian Future of Britishness conference of 14 January 2006. Have a go at identifying the Milton Model language and applying the appropriate Meta Model responses. Have fun.

> 'When we take time to stand back and reflect, it becomes clear that to address almost every one of the major challenges facing our country – our relationships with Europe, America and the rest of the world; how we equip ourselves for globalization; the future direction of constitutional change; a modern view of citizenship; the future of local government, ideas of localism; and, of course, our community relations and multiculturalism and, since July 7th, the balance between diversity and integration; even the shape of our public services – you must have a clear view of what being British means, what you value about being British and what gives us purpose as a nation.'

The language patterns of the Milton Model and Meta Model can be used in a variety of ways. There are no strict rules for when you should or should not use a particular pattern. It all depends on the outcome you want to achieve, your intention and your higher purpose. There will be times when artfully vague language will move you towards your outcome and times when the precision of the Meta Model is the most appropriate tool. However you decide to use these tools, take notice of the following health warning.

Using both types of language to excess will result in a severe breakdown of rapport. There is little else in this life as infuriating as someone who perpetually bombards you with the latest technique learned from a training course, and the Meta Model can have a particularly devastating effect. Practise these patterns with yourself as a continual challenge to your internal dialogue, and apply a high degree of subtlety when using them with other people. You can use your own words – whatever you are most comfortable with – it's your outcome that is important.

Frame your thinking

Frames are like aspects. If I look out of the front window of my house I get an aspect of the driveway and trees in the distance. If I look out of the back window I get an aspect of the garden and trees beyond.

Information frames are useful for thinking from different aspects. I will introduce you to six frames which I have found to be most useful, although there really is no limit on the types of frame which you could design for a particular context.

You can use information frames to clarify and focus either your own thinking or the thinking of a group, a client or an employee. Frames are used frequently to help keep meetings on track. Figure 7.3 shows six different frames.

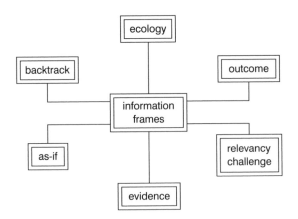

Figure 7.3 Information frames

Ecology frame

It is useful to switch to this frame when you sense ecological issues are being overlooked. This means being thoughtful of possible negative consequences in the wider system in which the issue under discussion is a part. So, for example, a suggested

product variation based on costs may have negative consequences on suppliers, customers, distributors and servicing.
Some questions to ask from within this frame would be:

■ What other consequences could there be if we make this
decision?

■ How will this decision affect the wider system?

■ Who else should we involve in this decision?

NLP is often referred to as 'the study of consequences', and the
ecology frame ensures that all consequences of an intention are
considered. Sometimes you may get an unsettling feeling about
a decision with no real evidence to back up a postponement.
This is your signal of incongruence cutting in and warning you
that something has been overlooked. A switch to the ecology
frame could avoid a potential future blunder.

Outcome frame

Outcomes were covered in detail in Chapter 3. The purpose of this
frame is to keep thinking focused on agreed aims while considering other possible outcomes. It is often necessary to remind
people of outcomes when activity begins to wander off track.

Relevancy challenge frame

At times it is important to keep full concentration on achieving
an outcome, and you may sense a comment or an action that
takes you off track. The relevancy challenge frame is similar to
the outcome frame in that its purpose is to maintain focus. The
relevancy challenge is used in an immediate way as soon as a
deviation is sensed.

Questions to ask are:

■ How does this/that help achieve the outcome?

■ What relevance does this/that have to the outcome?

Evidence frame

Sometimes you may find yourself, or your group, arriving at decisions without sufficient reason for doing so. In these situations the evidence frame will clarify your purpose and intention. This is a useful frame for improvement groups and problem solvers in general who need evidence with which to make comparisons between current and desired states. You will find the evidence frame useful for testing your own assumptions and actions. What evidence is there to determine how far you are from your outcomes?

As-if frame

The purpose of the as-if frame is to stimulate creativity. This is a useful frame where you have major personal decisions to make like job moves, additional roles or company moves. Visualising yourself as-if you have made the change by running the movie in your mind will help to highlight the part of the change that is generating the incongruence signal.

As-if frames are also ideal for creativity workshops and scenario planning sessions. The question to ask is, 'What could happen if … ?'

Backtrack frame

This frame is used to clarify understanding of previous information before proceeding further. It is used to deepen rapport through reflection of the words, tonalities and gestures used by others (these points will be covered in greater detail in the next chapter). It is also useful as a coaching tool to enhance the thinking of others.

For example, consider a coaching session where the outcome is to develop problem-solving abilities while working on a performance objective.

MANAGER: 'Tell me where you are on the (x) project.'

EMPLOYEE: 'I'm ready to approach the project board for an agreement to begin stage two.'

MANAGER: 'What do you need to do in order to achieve that?' (*backtrack*)

EMPLOYEE: 'Send them a detailed and costed plan.'

MANAGER: 'That's right – and what will you need to produce the plan?' (*backtrack*)

EMPLOYEE: 'I'll need resource allocation reports from engineering and up-to-date costs for materials and labour.'

MANAGER: 'How do you propose to go about getting them?' (*backtrack*) etc … etc … etc.

Reframe your thinking

To reframe is to change the meaning about something which causes a change in perception and attitude and opens up new possibilities. This is a powerful technique for which there are many examples in everyday business life – for example, the meeting with an unsettling authoritarian could mean that 'you interact from a defensive position with safety and survival in mind'. Reframed to mean 'a challenge to discover how much you can influence the person towards your ideas' would put you in a more resourceful state and would certainly influence your behaviour and therefore the outcome of the meeting.

A keynote speaker late for an important business conference walked on to the stage 45 minutes late and said, 'It's not that I'm late – I'm here as a result of foresight – you see my scheduled flight was delayed four hours, but luckily I decided to drive so that I could give my very sick neighbour a lift to the hospital. Had I taken my scheduled flight I would not be here at all, and perhaps neither would my neighbour. Thank you for your patience …'

Many business problems are divergent by nature, which can cause managers to suffer from the symptoms of stress. Albert Einstein's belief that 'in the middle of difficulty lies opportunity' offers these managers a superb reframe for divergent problem situations. Working with opportunities is much more rewarding than working with problems – and the attitude is much healthier too.

I have found enormous interest in reframing from my management students. It is often seen as a quick remedy for negativity and cynicism. Earlier you were introduced to a number of reframing examples, one of which was a reframe around the meaning of work. In one workshop we were dealing with the meaning of cynicism with a small group of managers who had been with the company for many years. Their problem was that *they had seen and heard it all before. It didn't work last time and it won't work this time. They're making decisions in the dark.* These were some of the phrases they were using.

They were not in a resourceful state for learning and they agreed it was because they were cynical about any change that top management introduced. I could have chosen to work with their meaning of work, but it was much easier working with their meaning of cynicism. I first got them all to agree that cynicism meant *they had seen it all before and showed little confidence in top management.* I then used a *higher chunk* within an *evidence frame* and a change of *perceptual position* to unsettle this meaning by saying, 'If you have little confidence in your top team, who by the way have demonstrated their ability to grow a successful company (higher chunk) which pays your wages and expenses every month (evidence), then who can you put your confidence in?' This rattled them a little as I continued with, 'And just imagine how the top team might interpret your cynicism (second perceptual position). What words do you think they might come up with for how you are reacting to their plans?'

Learn to learn with metaphor

> Prince Llewelyn lived in a castle. One day the prince went out, leaving his faithful and trusting dog Gelert to watch over his young son and protect him from the wolves roaming freely in the nearby forest. When the prince returned he found to his horror that his son was missing from his overturned cradle. There were bloodstains around the cradle and on the floor. He turned to find Gelert who was panting heavily with blood around his mouth. Distressed and fearing the worst, the prince drew his sword and stabbed Gelert through the heart. The prince's head dropped and his heart sank at what had happened, then from behind a curtain he heard a cry. It was his son, alive and well, standing next to the dead body of a wolf.

Metaphor is one of the earliest and most effective forms of learning. This story of Gelert the faithful dog can be used to teach the consequences of jumping to conclusions. The right metaphor, when told in an appropriate context, can deliver an extremely powerful learning message to the unconscious mind. Metaphors are memorable and can contain emotions as well as learning. Humour is ideally suited to metaphor. A great metaphor delivered well can lead an audience through many emotional states, from humour to heartbreak.

Is what you say congruent with what you do?

The notion of congruence has been referred to a number of times already in previous chapters. It is something that, like ecology, winds and twists around every element of NLP. It is important to cover congruence in the context of language because of the huge impact it can have on organisational effectiveness.

"Speak clearly, if you speak at all; Carve every word before you let it fall."

Dr Oliver Wendell Holmes (1809–94), American writer and physician

Often people don't seem to recognise when they are being incongruent. Yet other people pick up these signals unconsciously and respond accordingly. The director who sends all his managers on coaching and mentoring training, and yet continues to communicate in a dictatorial way, will transmit strong signals of incongruence between what he says and what he does.

Congruence requires a manager to become a paragon for others to follow. The old statements of leadership apply – lead by example, set standards for others, be a role model for others. If you are incongruent in your communication, then expect puzzling behaviour and low levels of performance from your employees. If you are congruent, accept the respect others will give to you.

08

Influence and persuasion

Business runs on decisions and interactions between people. From strategic decisions made by the board of directors to the decisions of managers and employees, the well-being of any organisation depends upon the quality of interaction and decision making.

"We are not won by arguments that we can analyse but by tone and temper, by the manner which is the man himself."

Samuel Butler (1835–1902), English author

Using rank to enforce compliance is an old-fashioned idea – a relic from Victorian times. Even the armed forces these days prefer to use modern motivation principles rather than rely on rank and authority. Compliance is fast being replaced by involvement and participation, and alongside this change in management style you have a change in influencing methods.

To belong to an organisation and have no influence over its operations is to be subservient to the ideas of others. 'Yes men' are like this – docile, passive and compliant. Business today needs fewer 'yes men' and more creative people who are prepared to take risks, try new angles and stretch the horizons of possibility. To do this requires a questioning mind, a passion for difference and change, and an ability to align others behind your thinking.

> **Business today needs fewer 'yes men' and more creative people who are prepared to take risks, try new angles and stretch the horizons of possibility.**

This kind of influence requires a respect for the other person's model of the world and really taking an interest in what other people do and say. It also needs integrity, patience and understanding. Without these qualities your attempts to influence others may be perceived as manipulative – in which case, your proposals are likely to fall on deaf ears. This brings us back to intention and purpose. If you have a worthwhile purpose with well-formed outcomes, and if your intention is biased towards the good of the business and not towards political gain, then you have the necessary basic principles for influencing *respectfully*.

> **To influence requires a respect for the other person's model of the world.**

Are you a trusting person?

People will allow themselves to be influenced by people they trust. This applies not only to the people you want to motivate in your team, but also to anyone you want to influence. People rarely buy from someone they don't trust. When interviewers are looking for the right person to fill a job role, they want to choose someone they feel they can trust. Job candidates with ideal experience and qualifications often get turned down because other candidates come across as more trusting.

Having integrity of purpose and honest intentions will be rewarded with trust, yet this is still not enough. There is a capability you can develop which is equally as fundamental and important as trust – 'being liked'. It is possible to trust someone and to dislike them, although trusting and liking are often closely linked. Do you have friends that you don't trust to return items you have loaned them? If a person *trusts* you and *likes* you, the basic requisites for influence are established.

> **Having integrity of purpose and honest intentions will be rewarded with trust.**

Liking and trusting is what happens between people when they have rapport with each other, and it can happen naturally or you can generate it intentionally.

Rapport

Building rapport is one of the most productive activities you can engage in. Having rapport makes everything so much easier. If one of your outcomes requires a certain person to cooperate or make a key decision, then I can think of nothing more outcome-oriented than rapport building with this person. In the same way that trust and liking can be generated intentionally, so can rapport.

So how do you go about gaining trust and getting people to like you? You simply be like them and show a sincere interest in them as a person. In any interaction, whenever you encounter resistance, it is a sign of a lack of rapport. Before I continue with the components of rapport, there are some key skills to master.

NLP

In any interaction, whenever you encounter resistance, it is a sign of a lack of rapport.

Sensory information

You have learned how behaviour provides cues to thought processes, and you know that beneath the surface of the words a person uses there are values, beliefs and metaprogrammes. Remember also that 55 per cent of someone's message is contained in their physiology and 38 per cent in their vocal qualities. Aside from the words used there is an enormous amount of information available that is vital in understanding, gaining trust, building rapport and gaining cooperation.

Sensory acuity

Gathering sensory information requires practice – and the act of practising is itself a rapport-building activity. You are showing an interest in people, and most people enjoy the experience of talking with someone who is interested in them. When you are being receptive to sensory information you need to have your attention focused entirely outside – this is called being in 'uptime' – totally alert with all your sensory receptors watching, listening, smelling, tasting and feeling the changes going on in the world around you. Being in 'downtime' is the opposite of this, where your attention is directed inside as you engage in reflective visualisation, internal dialogue or feeling. Whenever you are in downtime you are missing sensory evidence from the outside world.

It is often the most subtle changes that give the most significant cues to a person's thought process. Recently I asked an associate to take responsibility for a project. After discussing the implications he said, 'OK, I'm comfortable with that' – but I picked up a slight wavering in his voice. I didn't want to interrogate him so I just said, 'Actually it's not fair of me to foist this on to you just now – there are some loose ends which I should tidy up first.'

I didn't know what caused the wavering, but about three weeks later I learned that his knowledge of the project was very thin and he thanked me for retracting the responsibility which he originally accepted for the wrong reason. If you have ever persuaded someone to do something they didn't want to do, you are likely to have noticed a signal of incongruence from some part of their body language or voice tone. The words can say yes while, at the same time, the unconscious is saying no. The most important information about a person is their behaviour.

NLP

The most important information about a person is their behaviour.

Calibration

This is the term given to the act of noticing state changes in a person from behavioural cues such as posture, breathing, skin tone, expression and voice qualities. States are continually changing. It is easy to notice a change from smiling to crying – that doesn't take a tremendous amount of sensory acuity – but state changes are often more subtle than this.

Calibration is noticing exactly what you sense and nothing more. For example, you may be in a meeting and notice the chairman looking at you with a tightened forehead, reddish skin, fast breathing and with his fists clenched on the table. This is calibration. On the other hand, you might notice this behaviour and think 'he's upset about something – he's going to have a dig at me'. This is mind reading.

Pacing

If you were to sit outside on the pavement in a large town and watch people as they pass by, you would notice many differences between them. You would notice the speed at which their mind/ body rhythm is working, their pace, stride, breathing rate, facial expressions, eye movements and gestures. If you were to use a graph to represent the differences, you would end up with a range between two extremes (refer to Figure 8.1).

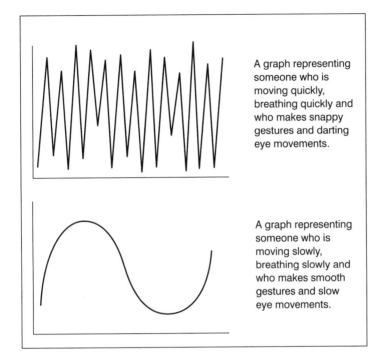

Figure 8.1 Extreme neurological states

Now, imagine putting together two people from each extreme. How would you describe their communication? Rapport would be out of the question while they are in such different neurological states from each other. For rapport to happen they will need to get rhythmically closer to each other.

Rapport can be developed simply by pacing various physical conditions. To pace someone's breathing is very powerful because of the link to the visual, auditory and kinaesthetic modalities (refer to Chapter 6). You can also pace body language by matching and mirroring.

Matching and mirroring

If you have ever watched people who have deep rapport with one another you will notice how closely their body posture, gestures and voice qualities are matched. Observe two lovers in a restaurant, or two people drinking at a bar, or a group of managers at a meeting. Matching is an unconscious form of communication that bonds relationships by deepening rapport. Matching is doing the same, i.e. sitting directly opposite someone, you match a lean to the right with a lean to your right. Mirroring is where you match their left with your right as a mirror image.

> **Matching is an unconscious form of communication that bonds relationships by deepening rapport.**

The intention of matching and mirroring is to communicate to a person's unconscious mind that you are on their wavelength. For example, imagine you want to influence a customer who is having a bad day and feeling low. It is important that you get his cooperation for your project, but he is slouching and talking in a negative way. To approach him confidently and ask him to get excited about your project may appear threatening. So, instead, pace his body language and voice characteristics. Avoid taking on his negative state by keeping in mind your intention to lead him to a position where he is motivated to work with you on your project. Your higher intention will keep you in a focused state. The intention behind an emotion is unconscious, while the intention to pace and lead is conscious.

When you are matching gestures, do so when it is your turn to speak, rather than when the other person is gesturing. A hunch of the shoulders, a hand on the breast, an open hand, a pointing finger – these are all unconscious communication gestures you can match or mirror. When matching the voice, listen for rhythm, volume, speed, tone and pitch. Fast talkers (strong visual people) are quickly frustrated by slow talkers (strong kinaesthetics) and slow talkers often find fast talkers difficult to follow. If you are highly visual, practise slowing down your speech by breathing more slowly. If you are highly kinaesthetic, practise speeding up your rate of speech.

Notice also the sensory words and phrases people use such as 'I *see* what you mean' and 'that *strikes* a chord' and match them. By using predicates from a person's preferred sensory system you are making yourself easy to listen to and understand. Build a vocabulary of predicates and practise matching them. Try mismatching a person's predicates and notice the response you get compared to when you are matching.

Pacing values

Anyone who has worked overseas in different cultures will realise the importance of values. As organisations evolve, they adopt cultural values that govern how people work. Some companies put a high value on time; others may value innovation more highly. The more accurately you can pace the really important values, the closer you will get to the person you are communicating with and the deeper your rapport will be. If you don't pick up a value from someone then simply ask them, 'What's important to you about this contract/product/relationship, etc.?' The reply will give you some of their values which you can refer to as you make your proposal or suggestion.

> **Values are hierarchical and vary in strength.**

Values are hierarchical and vary in strength. Chapter 1 explored how 'means' values are linked to higher-level 'end' values. The same is true for group values and personal values. In almost every case, when a choice must be made, group values will override personal values, although most people will join groups that have similar values to their own.

Metaprogrammes

Your metaprogrammes can be considered intrinsic values because of the value attached to thinking and behaving in certain ways. For example, a person who likes to work with procedures will value this in the nature of work and other activities they engage in.

There are words, gestures and other behavioural traits that indicate certain metaprogrammes. A person who is highly *away from*, for example, will talk about what they don't want much of the time. Someone with a *procedures* pattern will tend to count on their fingers and mark out sequences of events with their hands. A *through-time* person will check the time frequently, and someone with a *detail* pattern will give you much more detail than is necessary (unless you share the same pattern). An *others* person will often check with other people before taking an action, or in extreme cases not take the action at all for fear of upsetting someone.

These everyday simple signs that give away the underlying patterns of thinking can be used to match a pattern and build rapport. The danger in mismatching a pattern is that you can easily create confusion. Imagine a conversation between a big-picture person and a detail person and you will understand the stress that can be created in a relationship. By matching, you get closer to a person and create a greater sense of under-standing – remember it's the unconscious mind that feels more comfortable with the relationship when you do a good job of matching.

VAK

You can also match the modality a person is using to commu-nicate with you, whether visual (v), auditory (a) or kinaesthetic (k) or indeed any mix of these. It won't be important to do this with everybody, but it may give you the advantage you are looking for with someone you want to influence. You have already learned about eye-accessing cues, sensory words and physiological signs to indicate the modality being used, and any of these can be used to match a person's preferred style of communication. When you do this you create rapport. If you mismatch, as in visual vs kinaesthetic, you may be creating confusion at an unconscious level in the other person.

Leading

Pacing will build rapport, gain trust and convey a likeable personality. Once you have mastered the art of pacing, you can begin to influence people by leading them in the direction you want them to go. Some people are natural leaders and will hold a focal point while others seem content to follow. Your skill at pacing will put you in this same position, where others are content to follow you because they trust and like you. Of course, your proposals have to be sound – don't expect people to follow your lead if you are offering inappropriate plans.

The key to pacing and leading is a seamless transition. You can simply test whether you have paced sufficiently by adjusting your body posture and noticing if the other person follows you. If they do, you can continue to lead. If not, you need more rapport. I will go through some practical scenarios explaining how you might use pacing and leading, but first there is one more technique for your toolbag.

Anchoring

There are stories about soldiers who, years after serving in a war zone, run for cover upon hearing a car backfire. Their physiological reaction had been 'anchored' as an instant response to the sound of gunfire. Many of our everyday memories are anchored to external stimuli. The sound of a ringing bell can take you right back to your school days. The smell of cod-liver oil reminds me of my pre-school days where a spoonful a day was compulsory.

The external stimulus triggers an emotional state accessed from memory. Some of our anchors access pleasant emotions while others access unpleasant ones. Knowing about anchors, and how the process of anchoring works, allows you to use them to your advantage. You can use them with yourself to access specific states when you want them, and you can anchor states in other people. We all unconsciously anchor states in each other every day. I know of one manager who is very intelligent, experienced and professional in his role, and yet his boss, the managing director, has managed to anchor a state of subservience which is triggered by the sound of his voice over the telephone. There is a complete physiological shift from 'upright with head slightly down' to 'bent forward and hunched with the head slightly back'.

This is an example of an auditory anchor. A visual anchor might be a facial expression, a photograph or a picture. A kinaesthetic anchor might be a pat on the back or a squeeze of the hand. There are times when you may want to use some 'feeling good' anchors; at other times you may want to access states of 'creativity', 'focused analysis' or 'acute concentration'. How about anchoring your sixth strategy state to make it instantly accessible any time you want it?

You can set anchors in any modality – visual (v), auditory (a), kinaesthetic (k), olfactory (o) or gustatory (g); however, v, a and k anchors are more practical than o and g because with the latter you would have to carry a taste or smell around with you. The advantage of an anchor over other NLP techniques is that you can use it anywhere and at any time you may need it. The process for setting an anchor is simple:

1 Access the state you want to anchor.

2 Anchor the state with a unique stimulus (v, a, k or any combination).

3 Break state.

4 Fire your anchor (apply the same unique stimulus as in 2 above) and check with the strength of your inner feelings whether you have succeeded in creating the state change you wanted.

The key to successful anchoring is as follows:

1 **Uniqueness of the stimulus**   Combinations of voice tone, gesture and visuals work well. Imagine you are with a customer and you happen to catch her in a state of agreement over where to go for lunch. You could anchor this state by lowering your voice tone, pointing upward with your thumb and saying 'That's good'. At some later stage when you want a business decision, run exactly the same stimulus to access the agreement state as you say 'That's good' in the same voice tone, and at the same time as you raise your brow to suggest you are asking a question.

2 **Timing**   States vary in intensity and will rise to a peak before diminishing. Sometimes the rise and fall may be so fast that you miss it. This is where your sensory acuity comes in. You want to set your anchor just before the state peaks (refer to Figure 8.2 overleaf). Low-intensity states are not worth anchoring as they will not have the effect you desire. Anchor states that are worth accessing again. Here are some examples of states that might be worth accessing in others – agreement, enjoyment, concentration, creativity, relaxation, attention, learning and fun.

3 **Easy to repeat**   You may want to use an anchor more than once, so make your anchors easy to remember and repeat. Remember, it has to be unique, and when you use it you have to repeat exactly what you did when you first set it up. Standing on your head and singing may be unique, but how easy is it to repeat?

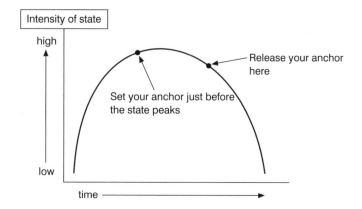

Figure 8.2 Applying an anchor – timing

The following examples include some of the techniques covered so far in this section with one or two additional techniques.

Example scenario 1: The negotiation

George is a manager negotiating with a supplier, Laura, and they are in the final stages of a tender to place a £2 million computer supply contract. George's outcome is to get Laura to drop her price to £1.6 million because she represents the preferred supplier whose bid price of £2 million is too much for the budget. Laura's outcome is to secure this contract for no less than 15 per cent below the bid price (£1.7 million). Laura is pacing and leading George.

GEORGE: 'Hello, Laura, it's good to see you again. How are you?'

LAURA: 'I'm fine. How are you, George?'

GEORGE: 'I'm digging around for cost savings I'm afraid.'

LAURA: 'That feels familiar. My household bills are piling up at the moment; I've simply got to tighten up somehow.'

(*Matching kinaesthetic predicates, the value of making cost savings, breathing, posture and voice qualities.*)

GEORGE: 'Well, let's get down to business. I am drawn to your
            proposal, and it went down well with the quality manager –
            but I must admit the overall cost was a shock. It overshoots
            our budget.'

LAURA: 'You know that we have never held back on quality before.
            It will always play a leading role in our service delivery. I am
            keen to explore how we can remove the shock – tell me,
            what would get you to feel more at ease with the
            proposal?'

(*Pacing the past and future, matching kinaesthetic predicates, breathing
and voice qualities. There is also an embedded suggestion, 'we can
remove the shock', which is marked out using a lower voice tone. Laura
ends by asking a question with the purpose of accessing a 'feel good'
state which she will attempt to anchor.*)

GEORGE: 'Cut the price by 50 per cent and invoice in arrears?'

(*This is a half-serious answer made with a light-hearted laugh which is
turned into a question by a higher voice tone at the end.*)

LAURA: 'I like clients with a sense of humour like you, George.
            How would you feel if I were to cut the cost by say 12.5
            per cent, which I could do by reducing part of the
            service?'

(*The words* 'I like' *were emphasised by volume and tone at the same
time as she tapped her fingers sharply on the desk – this combination set
up a unique auditory stimulus anchor for George's light-hearted laugh.
More value matching at the personal level (sense of humour) with the
initial sentence.*)

GEORGE: 'That's moving in the right direction, but I was hoping
            for more than 12.5 per cent; can you move any
            further?'

(*George is persistent but happy to be led by Laura because the rapport is
so good. He is enjoying himself.*)

LAURA: 'I can move a little further, I have always managed to accommodate you in the past, haven't I? I will have to review the services though. Let me recap for a moment. I know you don't expect me to compromise on quality, and yet you want a reduction in excess of 12.5 per cent. I could revise the service offering to reduce our costs, but that would be a compromise on the service to your customers. I feel sure that, like me, you would rather compromise on the price than on quality or service (fires anchor). I am happy to offer you 14 per cent right now on the proposal as it stands with no compromise on quality and service. Can we strike a deal on this now?'

(More matching and pacing. Leading begins when Laura starts to recap. Lots of matching values – quality and service. More rapport building with the words 'I feel sure that, like me', which contains an embedded suggestion 'like me'. The question 'haven't I?' is tagged on to the end of a sentence intentionally to get George to say the word 'yes', which is an agreement state. Laura fires her anchor by using the same voice tone that was used to set the anchor as she taps the table in the same place to make the same sound. The anchor is fired to access George's light-hearted laugh state, just as she begins to make her final offer.)

Example scenario 2: The inquest

Jeff is a service manager being called to explain a major service incident by his client, Mike, whose outcome is to give Jeff a hard time and keep him in an underdog position. Jeff's outcome is to use the meeting as an opportunity to build rapport and strengthen their relationship. Jeff is pacing and leading Mike.

MIKE: 'Hello, Jeff. Sit down. Coffee?'

JEFF: 'Yes please.'

MIKE: 'I have to say that this incident is possibly the worst on record and I will need a complete account of what happened. I also want to be assured that you are capable of preventing any future occurrence.'

JEFF: 'The incident has been clearly documented in this report. You'll find it contains complete details of what happened, which I am very happy to discuss with you.'

(*Jeff has avoided taking a defensive position, given Mike what he asked for, and paced his auditory predicates, breathing, posture and voice qualities.*)

MIKE: 'What do you have to say to reassure me, and my colleagues, that your organisation is capable of supplying us with a consistent service that complies with our standards?'

JEFF: 'We have always listened consistently to your needs and complied with your requests for additional services. I want to state my concern over this one incident, and at the same time assure you, and your colleagues, that we will remain tuned in to the standards written in the service criteria which were established when we first signed the contract.'

(*Pacing values of consistency and standards, chunking up from the incident to 'service criteria', matching predicates, breathing, posture and voice qualities.*)

MIKE: 'Well, that's true; perhaps this incident was caused by human error, in which case there is still no excuse for what happened.'

JEFF: 'The report clearly explains the cause, and you are right, I am not going to give you excuses. And you know, there have been five problems in total this year which we dealt with effectively. On a contract of this size and complexity overall performance is our aim, and as you said, we are meeting the overall service criteria. We have achieved this by listening and adapting our service as the requirements have changed. This incident has been taken seriously, as you will see from the detail in the report, and we are already writing new procedures from what we have learned.'

(More matching of predicates and pacing of values. Jeff begins to pace the conversation here as he slowly changes his posture, voice tone and gestures to strengthen his words, which have moved focus from the incident to higher-level values, achievement, procedures and learning.)

"What you do speaks so loud that I cannot hear what you say."

Ralph Waldo Emerson (1803–82), American essayist, poet and philosopher

In extreme examples where someone is really against you, patience is the key. Just keep matching, mirroring and pacing and you will eventually get rapport to a level at which you can begin to lead.

The next chapter will draw on what you have read up to this point and introduce you to many more ways of using NLP in common business situations. The techniques included in Chapter 9 have been chosen for their effectiveness in the context presented, and they all have the same outcome – *to help you achieve a personal competitive advantage!*

09

Applying NLP to 10 everyday challenges

You have now covered the basic concepts and dynamics of NLP and applied them in various exercises dealing with the key themes of being an effective manager and leader. In this chapter you will learn how to apply NLP to everyday challenges using a variety of different techniques and exercises. I trust that, by now, you have realised that NLP has such a wide application, limited only by the blocks to your own creative thinking. While this chapter is meant to be one you can dip into when you need it, some of the exercises refer to earlier parts of the book for a fuller description of the techniques suggested.

NLP and stress management

The process of getting stressed is something you learn. How stressed you get will depend on how well you have learned to tense your muscles, frown, have negative internal dialogue and dark murky mental imagery, and breathe rapidly from your upper chest. You will also have learned when to get stressed, such as times when you are late for a meeting and get stuck in traffic, or when you sense time is running out and your tasks are nowhere near completion; perhaps other people are being difficult or producing poor-quality work or maybe your boss is putting you under increasing pressure. It could be that you are not meeting your own very high standards of work. Maybe things just aren't going to be perfect, right or as you want them to be. Whatever triggers your stress, know that you have learned to create it for yourself. Although stress is often related to the environment, it has really more to do with your ability to control your response to potentially stressful situations.

Exercise 9.1: Conquering stress

Here's a way of dealing with stress using both mind and body.

Mind

Bring to mind a situation that tends to get you stressed. Focus on the next time you will be in this situation and create an image of the scenario. See yourself in the image as you are responding to the stressful situation, but this time you will be responding differently – in a more calm and controlled way, disconnected emotionally from whatever is going on around you. As you watch this image, tell yourself how ridiculous it was that you used to get stressed and how much better you feel now you are in control of your reaction. Turn up the brightness, colour and contrast of your image, and adjust any sound so that it makes you feel even more in control and relaxed. Bring your image closer and notice how the feelings of calm and control get stronger.

Body

Continue to focus on your image and breathe deeply in a relaxed and natural way. Inhale all the way down to your lower abdomen while relaxing your body, paying particular attention to your shoulders, jaw and brow. Inhale and exhale through your nose.

As you continue to breathe deeply and naturally, look down and tell yourself how easy it is to be relaxed no matter what is going on around you; after all, life is full of potentially stressful situations but you needn't get emotionally tangled in them – now you are in control and can focus on what's really important, not on how you are feeling.

Return to the image you have created in your mind and put a frame around it. Now push it off into the distance so you can just make out some of the detail. As you observe the situation from this distance, being fully relaxed and in control, project these feelings into your image and bring it closer, and as it comes towards you, strengthen the feelings of calm and control. Allow the image to come so close that you become part of the image, fully associating with it and the powerful feelings of calm and control. Just as the feeling begins to peak, squeeze together the thumb and middle finger of your left hand, hold for about 20 seconds and then release. You have now set yourself an anchor which you can use any time you are faced with a potentially stressful situation.

Stress is damaging to both mind and body, and you owe it to yourself to take care of your stress levels. Remember also that for some people stress can be a driver. We may never achieve anything without feeling under some degree of stress. It's when stress starts to make you tired, tense, fatigued and achy that it gets dangerous. If the stress isn't firing you up and you don't feel great, then you need to address it.

NLP and time management

Noticing the language we use to describe time gives clues about the way we allow time to act upon our experience metaphorically. Some of these metaphors are quite ridiculous. Here are some common ones with their presuppositions:

- *I haven't got time for that* (time is a possession – something you have or haven't got)
- *I can't make the time to do that* (time can be manufactured)

- *There's never enough time* (time is a commodity which is always in short supply)
- *Time is against us* (time has physical form and energy)
- *Time is on our side* (time can choose to take sides)
- *We have all the time in the world* (time is contained by the world and we can own it)
- *Time waits for no one* (time is inconsiderate).

These common metaphors are used to express a relationship with time. It may seem harmless to say these things, but the language you use has a real effect on your behaviour. Metaphors like these are perceptual filters on your engagement with time. The way you relate to time through metaphor has an immediate influence on your level of productivity and effectiveness.

Think how absurd the title of this section is. As if anyone can actually manage time! It's one of the few things we have no influence over whatsoever. So, instead of trying to manage time, think of using the time you have more effectively. This has little to do with lists and schedules and everything to do with emotions and the conscious awareness of how much activity is required for any particular task, and how much time each task will take.

Emotions and priorities

Make a list of tasks that are part of your role as manager and categorise them into those tasks you enjoy and those you don't – for whatever reason. As you look down your list, is it apparent where you are losing time? It will be because of one of the following three factors:

- You have not learned to delegate your tasks to others.
- You spend more time than is necessary on tasks you enjoy.
- You spend more time thinking about tasks you don't enjoy than getting on with them.

I am using the term *enjoy* quite loosely here – another way of categorising is to select one group of tasks that you just get on with and another group that you tend to keep at a mental and emotional distance because you're unsure how best to handle them. In fact, this is what tends to happen and why time management is more about emotions than lists of important things to do. What do you do when you have prioritised your tasks for the week and on Monday morning you get an email asking you for two hours of your time to attend a meeting which you hoped you wouldn't have to attend? You need to deal with more than just priorities, as these will continue to shift on a weekly, if not daily and sometimes hourly, basis. You also need to manage the emotional distance between you and your tasks so that you can get on with things and stop pushing tasks to the back of your mind. When you are fully engaged, it's amazing how much you can get done.

Emotional distance can be caused by any of the following:

- You find the people you have to deal with difficult, awkward or puzzling.

- You find part or all of the task confusing, difficult or boring.

- You are uncertain about the value of putting effort into the task.

- You have certain beliefs about your relationship with the task or the people you must deal with.

Now take each one of the tasks from your 'mental and emotional distance' category and identify what it is about the task that is causing you to create the distance. Once you have identified the cause, write it down and, as you are writing, notice the state you are in. Chances are you will be in an unresourceful state and this is what is really stopping you from cracking on with these tasks. If you could get rid of the task, you would probably have done so by now, so by default the tasks in your list are ones you feel you *have to* do. If this is so, then isn't it better to be in a resourceful state when thinking about them, and doing them? When you are in a positive state you simply do a better job, so find something to get into a positive state about.

This not *that*

One way to recognise where you may be using time ineffectively is to listen for the words *this* and *that* when referring to tasks. These small words can give an insight into the degree of emotional and mental connection with each of your tasks. In normal everyday use we tend to use the word *that* when referring to something distant, either in time or location – for example, '**that** project we did last year' compared with '**this** project I am doing now', and '**that** office across town' compared with '**this** office we are working in here'. The word *that* is also used to keep mentally and emotionally distanced from a task that is current – for example, '**that** project he is managing' or 'I have to do **that** job now'. It tends to be used when the project or task is something we are not looking forward to for some reason. Pay attention also to the type of emotion connected with the word *this* since a negatively charged *this* can be devastating to performance as well – for example, 'I'm getting hacked-off with **this**.'

Keeping a mental distance from a problem can be very useful when it is done with a clear intention of problem solving; however, when you are distanced in this context you can be certain that you will be less focused and will have to fight distraction to get the job done. You are likely to procrastinate and waste time with tasks you refer to as *that* more than those you refer to as *this*. The next time you catch yourself using *that* to refer to tasks which are current, ask yourself, 'Am I really focused on doing a great job? What is causing me to make it a *that*?' Then do the following exercise and get yourself into an appropriately positive state for getting on with the task in hand, whoever the project manager happens to be.

Exercise 9.2: Motivate yourself to get things done

Take one *that* task and begin to look for the positive benefits to you that would result from getting the task done effectively. Write down each positive benefit you identify. Look deep for positive benefits you may not have recognised before. You want to find all the positive benefits in doing this task. Perhaps the task you are thinking of right now will provide you with some sort of challenge or stretch. Maybe it's an opportunity to learn something new or build a relationship. There is always something of benefit in everything if you look long enough and are prepared to reframe your perception.

Next go through the 'well-formed outcomes' procedure in Chapter 3 to ensure you have everything you need to do a great job, and then create positive, empowering images of success in your mind. Use your imagination to make the image bright and clear. See all the positive benefits of getting this task done. Make your image bigger and bring it closer to you. How do you feel about *this* task now? Do the same thing for other tasks in the same category, creating more energy and motivation for getting you engaged with the task.

How useful is your personal time code?

How you code time and relate to it is a major influence on how you use the time you have. People who use their time productively have a good sense of the passing of time and how long a minute, hour or three hours really is. It's the reason why some people are consistently late and others are always on time. Your personal 'time code' occupies the physical space around your body. Albert Einstein discovered the link between space and time, and we now know how individuals relate to time (refer to the section on time in Chapter 2). People with a *through-time* pattern, or code, will know where and when they have to be and are likely to spend time preparing. An *in-time* pattern, or code, will have the opposite effect, putting the owners in various states of chaos and uncertainty as they rush between appointments, being habitually late.

If you have an *in-time* code that isn't helping, how do you go about changing it? The answer is to design yourself a 'being on time and prepared' strategy and timeline. So prepare to spend longer thinking about how much time things really take and how important certain activities really are.

Exercise 9.3: Focus on what's really important to you

Begin by identifying what is really important to you (refer to the section on values in Chapter 1), and choose a couple of activities related to one of your top priorities from this list. For each activity, set yourself an outcome and mentally rehearse what you will need to do to achieve it. Think about what preparation you want to do and calculate an estimated amount of time for each task you have identified.

Now, look down to your left and tell yourself how much more you will be achieving now you have this new strategy, then look up to your right and see how much more effective you are being. Notice how you are bringing conversations to a close so you can move on to other more pressing activities, and how you are taking the time to be well prepared for your meetings. Now look down to your right and enjoy the feeling of being in control. Look down again to your left and repeat this cycle of down-left to tell, up and right to see, down and right to feel at least five times until your mind becomes familiar with the idea that you are going to be working in a different way from now on, focused on the activities that are going to move you closer to your outcomes.

Timeline

You can now make the strategy even more powerful by designing a new timeline. First of all, imagine a timeline that starts with this moment 'now' right in front of you and moves out to your past at a 45-degree angle to your left, and to your future at a 45-degree angle to your right. The line can stretch out away from you as far as you want it to. Make your new timeline brightly coloured and distinct in some way so it is pleasing to look at. Now take each task in turn from the previous exercise and capture it as a still image, brightly coloured, clear and in a frame. Continuing to work with your imagination, place this image at a point on your timeline in the future where you think it will be happening. Do this for all the other tasks and remember to refer to your new timeline frequently over the next few weeks until it becomes habitual. Your new 'being on time and prepared' strategy is now complete.

Here is a classic NLP exercise working with timeline and visualisation which can be used for creating successful future events.

Exercise 9.4: Planning for success

Is there a task coming up in the future that is important to you, your team or your organisation, and at which you want personally to excel? Perhaps an important meeting, a planning session with your team, a customer presentation, a strategic report you have to write, a full blown multi-million pound project or a job interview? You are going to use a spatial metaphor to help build a successful event, so you will need plenty of physical space for this exercise.

Step 1

Imagine that your future timeline projects out in front of you on to the floor – as if you are rolling out a red carpet.

Step 2

Place an image of you succeeding in this future task on the timeline at a distance that feels right to you. Make the image a bright colourful one. The image can be on any plane, it can be 3-D and with sound effects if you like.

Step 3

Now walk down your timeline, stop when you are on top of your image and become fully associated with the feeling of success in this task. Feel how good it is to be this successful. Enjoy this feeling for a few moments.

Step 4

Continue walking now, just past your image. Stop and turn around so that you are looking down your timeline back to the *now* point. You should be focusing on the time between *now* and your image of success (refer to Figure 9.1). As you focus your

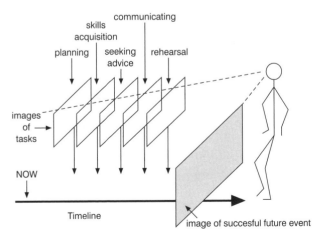

Figure 9.1 Building success into future events

thinking on this time span, imagine all the things you had to do to ensure your success. Here are some examples of useful questions to focus your thinking:

1 What was important to you?

2 What plans did you have to make?

3 Who did you inform about your task?

4 Who did you communicate with?

5 What method of communication was most relevant?

6 Did you need extra skills – and how did you acquire them?

7 Was advice from experienced and successful people helpful to you?

8 Did you rehearse and/or practise?

What you are doing at this stage is visualising, having done all the things you needed to do in order to achieve a successful task. When you are comfortable that everything has been considered, you can begin to fit them on to your timeline in the places that seem most appropriate.

Step 5

When you have all your images in place on your timeline, you are ready to walk back to the original *now* position that you started from, pausing momentarily over each image to fully associate into the activity. When you arrive back at your original position and look down your timeline, are you confident that each of the tasks you have identified is sufficiently detailed to ensure your success? If the answer is *yes*, you have completed the exercise. If you have any doubt or uncertainty, then take another walk down your timeline until you get to the place where the doubt is generated and make whatever adjustments you consider necessary.

This process will give you feedback about the reality of your planned time allocation for completing the task. Have you invested sufficient time in all the necessary areas in order to ensure you achieve your outcome, without any question of doubt? The questions above are provided as examples only and are certainly not exhaustive. You may find your own questions more relevant to your particular chosen task.

> "Time goes, you say? Ah, no! Alas, Time stays; we go."
>
> Austin Dobson (1840–1921), British author

This technique can be used to build success into any future task, and it is particularly useful for major events. Timeline planning, particularly for important projects, is a very thorough and effective process. Used in conjunction with other NLP techniques it enables you to build robustness, certainty and accomplishment into your future.

NLP and personal creativity

> "Imagination is not a talent of some men, but is the health of every man."
>
> Ralph Waldo Emerson (1803–82), American essayist, poet and philosopher

Every creation began its life as a thought in one person's mind, but not all mind creations make it into the physical world. This takes execution. The result of a well-executed creative idea is innovation. It is common for many people to have a creative idea, but only one person may have what it takes to execute and innovate. Throughout the book you have been introduced to new ways of thinking that can really change how you behave and how you feel. If you have restricted yourself to the reading, without executing the exercises, it is unlikely you will change anything. NLP works well when you do the exercises, and the result is new and innovative ways of relating to the world.

The Nobel prize winner Linus Pauling said, 'The best way to have a good idea is to have lots of ideas.' Creative thinking is the pathway to innovation, but to innovate you need to execute just one idea.

Everyone has the ability to think creatively and to innovate, but some people find this difficult because they have unconsciously erected barriers that block their thinking.

The best way to have a good idea is to have lots of ideas.

Hindrances to creativity and innovation

Here is some guidance on how to overcome the major hindrances to creative thinking and generation of innovative ideas.

Step out of your habitual thinking

Have you noticed that, where a job requires quick thinking and where time is at a premium, sometimes the tendency to find a solution too quickly ends up creating another problem? You can recognise this when you hear problems being described as solutions.

An example of this is where you might be restricted in your ability to increase production because the machinery is running at capacity. To say 'we need to invest in more production machinery' is to define a solution, and in doing so blocks any other possible solutions from being created. It is more useful to say 'we are producing to capacity with this machinery' and open up the potential for creating a wider choice of solutions – for example, contracting the extra work out, utilising seasonal fluctuations in demand or reducing the amount of rework.

Habitual thinking limits perspective (refer to Figure 9.2). You can widen perspective on a problem by adopting different ways of thinking about it.

You can widen perspective on a problem by adopting different ways of thinking about it.

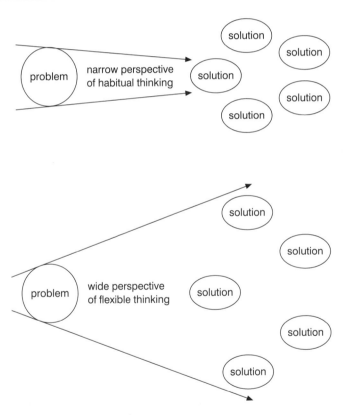

Figure 9.2 Perspective

Step outside the problem

Have you ever watched a group of eleven-year-olds playing football? They become so totally involved in the action that they all follow the ball wherever it goes. There is no plan other than to get the ball, kick it in the general direction of the goal and follow it. It is only when they grow older that they discover team tactics and strategy.

To see alternative solutions and new perspectives requires a certain degree of mental distance from the problem. Pull back from the problem, take a meta perspective and you will be able to make lots of new connections and generate fresh ideas around the problem scenario you are dealing with.

Make your beliefs and values work for you

Contrary to what some people may believe, the marketing people don't have a monopoly on ideas. Neither do artists, poets, scientists or film directors. Everyone has the ability to create and be innovative, and the first place to begin making improvements is to examine your beliefs. If you believe you are not creative, or that your creativeness has limitations, then that's exactly what you are likely to live up to.

> **Everyone has the ability to create and be innovative.**

A limiting belief can block you from developing your creative thinking styles – so change it to a belief that will support and encourage you to widen your perspectives on problems. It is also worth checking out your identity and values. If being creative isn't important to you, it is unlikely that you will put energy into developing your creative capability. Likewise, if you don't connect with innovation in some way as part of your identity, this will severely hinder creativity.

What does your culture value most – creative thinking or action?

Creativity and innovation require curiosity for which there is a language – the language of questions. There is another language in organisations – the language of action. Notice what people say and how often each type of language is used. The two languages can be related to the early metaphor in Chapter 1, where the action language is used by people responding with *defeat*, *reaction* and *complexity*, while the language of questions is used by people responding with *curiosity*. Which type of language do you use?

Which type of language do you use?

The language of action consists of dialogue that is about doing, achieving, analysing, evaluating, utility and necessity. The language of curiosity is less concrete, and more to do with contemplation, imagination and possibility. There is a place and time for both these languages, but in some organisations action alone is rewarded, so people spend all their time doing and little time thinking and being curious.

Types of problems in organisations

I will emphasise two main categories of problem – convergent and divergent.

Convergent problems

Many day-to-day operational problems seem complicated and ambiguous on a first appraisal, but really all they need is a logical thought process to solve them. These problems are contained within a relatively small part of the overall organisational system, and they can be neatly funnelled towards a specific solution. For example, suppose information coming in from clients using a variety of services is getting broader, and this is making it difficult to find exactly what you are looking for and to channel it into the marketing effort. One solution would be to categorise the information types and build a search function to access it using special software.

Divergent problems

Divergent problems tend to be influenced by more than one business unit, and the more you attempt to apply a logical thought process the more divergent the problem becomes, often moving off into many different directions, making it difficult to represent as one entity. Consider the following situation.

Example: Resistance to change

Employees in the service division of a communications company seem not to be interested in improving the quality of operational processes. They work hard and they get on well as a team but appear content to continue working with inadequate methods and procedures. They think that managers, not themselves, are responsible for fixing things. The division has been struggling to maintain service levels and is now showing signs of resistance to the demand for improvements from management and from clients. Whatever managers tried to fix the problem, it just popped up somewhere else. These types of problems can have multiple causes which are not so obvious or apparent on surface inspection.

This is a typical divergent problem. There may be many reasons why people resist change, and there could be any number of different dynamics acting all at the same time with no logical or rational reason. A common response to these problems is the *complexity* response – investing resources into designing and implementing comprehensive management, measurement and improvement systems. Sometimes management changes and training are sought for a quick solution. Often the fundamental problem remains because the response provided a solution when what was needed was more curiosity to understand the root causes of the problem.

People are the backbone of any organisation. It is possible to consider changes to processes in the confines of an executive meeting room without considering the influence of people, but to do so is myopic. Listening, understanding and involvement are the oil on the wheels of change.

Managers who invest time in productive two-way, face-to-face communication with people will pick up messages from physiology that are not contained in words. Many divergent problems are complicated because people are involved and they often have different and sometimes conflicting priorities. If you remove people from the equation, many organisational problems become convergent. Consider this simple scenario.

Example

A manager decides that it would be a great PR exercise for all employees to wear badges saying 'Total Quality Commitment'. The manager gets everyone together and says, 'I want you all to wear these badges as a sign to our customers that we are committed to quality.' What actually happens is that the badges are worn – but only when the manager visits them.

In this case, the manager in question didn't have the sensory acuity to pick up from nonverbal responses that there was a problem with wearing the badges. Not only that, but the issue isn't really about badges, it's about the way they are treated by managers generally. These signs will only be picked up by managers who are sensitive to them and understand the nature and importance of motivation. Noticing these nonverbal cues of dissatisfaction will increase your flexibility to deal with underlying divergent problems such as this one.

The wearing or non-wearing of badges may seem insignificant, and in isolation it is. However, it brings to the surface the much deeper problem of mutually uncooperative manager/employee relationships. If this issue were to be addressed, it could have a much wider influence on significant areas like productivity, efficiency and effectiveness.

Daydream your way to success

Albert Einstein and Walt Disney were both endowed with creative genius.[1] They both had very well-developed visual modalities, and they both spent a great deal of time daydreaming – engrossed in their inner movies. Einstein's early memory, which led to his Theory of Relativity, was of a daydream during a mathematics class where he visualised himself sitting on a beam of light. Einstein had the sensory acuity to notice that his thoughts were born from images. He developed his visual modality by suppressing words and thinking in pictures alone, which removed boundaries to his imagination. Walt Disney used strong imagery to conjure up exciting new cartoon films, and he also used sound and movement to create, in his mind, the full VAK experience for his audience.

Visualising is very useful for thinking about divergent problems. Language can constrain possibility. Yet, in many organisations, particularly those focused on action and reaction, you are unlikely to win favour by staring out of the window. The ability to 'think on your feet' is applauded, and mastering this ability can make you appear highly dynamic; however, the quality of decisions made 'on the hoof' will depend upon the ability to switch styles of thinking in the midst of action. Your ability to do so will depend on your existing ability to visualise and getting enough practice to make it a habit.

The next exercise is based upon Walt Disney's creativity strategy, which will be explained in more detail in the next section of this chapter. With practice, this exercise will help you to be more creative, innovative and decisive 'on your feet'.

Exercise 9.5: Thinking on your feet

This strategy can be used in any situation requiring creative solutions to a problem being discussed. The context is not important.

1 Picture the situation and construct possible solutions in your mind's eye. Let your imagination roam free – it's OK to be different and unorthodox. Adopt the dreaming posture (head slightly up and cocked to left, eyes up-right). Proceed to step 2 after having created a number of possible solutions.

2 Criticise each visual idea using internal dialogue. Adopt the critical evaluation posture (head slightly down, left hand on chin, index finger pointing up towards ear, eyes down-left). What are the advantages and disadvantages of each possibility?

3 Imagine you have decided to go with a solution. What does it feel like to have accepted it? Does it feel right? Test for incongruence signals. Adopt the reality posture (relax, head slightly down, eyes down-right, breathe from lower abdomen).

4 If in step 3 you feel incongruent about the solution, repeat steps 1–3 using fresh visual ideas as the content.

5 If in step 3 you feel congruent, repeat steps 1–3 with your solution as the content. If in step 3 you still feel congruent the second time around, trust your solution and decide now!

There is a variation to this pattern in which you may want to choose between two ideas. What you do is to construct a clear image in your mind of each solution side by side at some point in the distance, and flit your eyes from one to the other looking for differences. The other steps are the same – take the solution which appears to be most appropriate and put it through the auditory and kinaesthetic processes. This is more like a decision-making process than a creative one, but it is extremely useful for making decisions 'on the hoof'. It is worth practising this strategy, as it is possible to develop it so that the whole process can be completed within a few seconds. You will notice people who do this naturally as their eyes flit rapidly between two locations of focus.

Natural creative you

Everyone has a unique state they put themselves into when they are being creative. Like everything else, your level of creativity will be state dependent. A high-intensity state of creativity will produce more and better ideas than a low-intensity state. Therefore it makes sense to calibrate an intense state and anchor it for future access. This is particularly useful when you need to be creative for extended periods like brainstorming sessions and visualising futures.

Recall a specific time when you were being highly creative. If nothing comes to mind, it's OK to imagine what it would be like to be highly creative. Now take this memory and visualise what you look like as you are being creative. See yourself being highly creative, and hear what you are saying and what others around you are saying. Make the picture brighter, bigger and more colourful. Turn up the sound, pan it from left to right, then have it continue in a circle all the way around. Make the picture even bigger and three-dimensional. Exaggerate movement and bring it towards you as you associate with it. Be aware of your feelings inside and anchor this state by pressing your temples with the middle finger of each hand just before your state reaches its peak of intensity. Choose a different place on your body to set the anchor if you prefer. The important thing is to make sure it's a location you can find again with a good degree of precision when you want to fire the anchor.

Repeat this exact-same process, with exactly the same anchor four or five times, making sure that you 'break state' between each one. The result will be an anchored, high-intensity state of creativity which you can access whenever you want to boost a future creative thinking process. The best time to anchor this state, or any state, is when you are experiencing it in the real world, so the next time you find yourself being highly creative, anchor the state.

Regenerate your flow

Have you ever been in a state of intense concentration and suddenly got blocked? It could be that you were writing an important letter and found yourself stuck for a particular word or phrase. It could be a convergent problem that required careful, logical thought, and your flow of thinking got blocked somehow. What actually happens in these instances is that the chemicals in your brain create neural connections that seem to get welded together. What you need to do is break these connections to allow new and different connections to be made.

The brain, which has two halves – left and right – works through a complex and countless number of neural linkages. The left side of the brain processes information sequentially, one chunk at a time, and it controls the right side of the body. The right side processes whole pieces of information and controls the left side of the body.

This information will help to explain the nature of the next exercise. It works by forcing you to use both sides of your brain simultaneously. The exercise comes from kinesiology and is used to help balance left and right brain activity to break habitual brain patterns and force new connections to be made. Since the mind is not so good at unblocking itself, you can use the body instead. This exercise will unblock the severest of stuck thinking by scrambling the neural connections! Notice the difference between how you feel inside your head before and after the exercise.

Exercise 9.6: Scrambling the brain

A$_L$	B$_R$	C$_L$	D$_T$	E$_R$
F$_L$	G$_T$	H$_R$	I$_R$	J$_L$
K$_T$	L$_R$	M$_L$	N$_T$	O$_R$
P$_L$	Q$_T$	R$_L$	S$_R$	T$_L$
U$_L$	V$_R$	W$_T$	X$_R$	Y$_T$

Refer to the diagram and starting at the top left, follow the alphabet through to Y and back again. Say each letter of the alphabet out loud at the same time as doing the following actions:

L = raise left arm and right foot
R = raise right arm and left foot
T = raise both arms and stand on tip-toe

This exercise can be modified for the office and done discreetly at your desk by using internal dialogue and raising fingers and toes. Once you have used this pattern a few times it will start to become habitual. Prevent this by mixing up the letters L, R and T to produce different patterns.

I hope you found the exercise fun and effective … try it when you really get stuck for the answer to a problem. Other movements to get your mind to change include juggling, mini-basketball, skipping, pogo, stretching – anything to get the blood pumping through your veins. The main thing is to move your body if you want to move your mind.

Supercharge your creativity

How you enhance your own state of creativity will be unique to you. Whether you work at improving your visual, auditory or kinaesthetic modalities will depend upon your current preference. Recent brain research has shown that creativity and learning can be enhanced by stimulating the brain in a number of different ways – emotionally, nutritionally and physically/mentally.

In the mood for creativity

The brain learns best when it is emotionally charged, either negatively or positively. People easily recall emotional highs and lows in their life. Negative emotions create stress and so are not conducive to creativity. There is also a strong tendency to suppress negative or unpleasant emotions. It is better to create an environment where informality, humour and freedom of expression are acceptable.

Formal business environments stifle creativity. Music is a powerful way of accessing positive emotional states. Many of our positive emotional experiences will be anchored to particular songs or tunes. Music which relaxes and helps to generate positive emotions will also enhance creative thinking.

NLP and group creativity

The ability to choose your own creative thought process is something you have complete control over. This is not so with groups. Most will require at the minimum some form of facilitation or structural framework and training to help them break out of habitual problem/solution processes.

"The world we have made as a result of the level of thinking we have done thus far creates problems that we cannot solve at the same level at which we have created them … We shall require a substantially new manner of thinking if humankind is to survive."

Albert Einstein (1879–1955), American physicist

Quality circles and other such improvement initiatives are formal structures for helping teams to think creatively about problems. Brainstorming is the most common form of group creativity process used in organisations today, and for many problems it is reasonably effective as a high-level process.

The key question

Among the many questions that will be asked during a problem-solving activity, there is one key question:

What type of problem is this?

This question moves you to a higher level from where it is possible to get a clearer picture.

For example, a production line is having trouble matching its output to sales forecasts. Sometimes output exceeds requirement and at other times it falls short. There are many arguments between production supervisors and sales about poor communication, inaccurate orders on the computer system and last minute changes to order specifications. As the company grows and sales orders get larger and more complex, the problems become more severe and diverse, with stress and frustration leading to decreased motivation and lower levels of productivity.

> **The words you use to define a problem will influence your solution.**

The words you use to define a problem will influence your solution. What type of problem is this? It could be classed as a problem of motivation, skill shortage, attitude, communication, process, systems, timing or any number of other seemingly obvious categories. How you define the problem situation will determine where you look for solutions.

Sources of problems

The sources of problems can be diverse, but as far as NLP is concerned, if the people working in the system are motivated to work together to achieve greatness as a team, then even the most complex of problems can be solved and turned into amazing new opportunities. So any problem solving that involves more than one person has the potential for creating brilliant possibilities as long as the people involved are working cooperatively towards the same goal. Problem solving in teams then focuses on systems thinking and the team dynamics as a fundamental requirement to creating solutions.

How do you see the problem?

When activity is driven by perceptions rather than what is actually happening you are not problem solving but guessing and mind reading.

A manager inherited a large and politically difficult on-site computer service contract which, under previous management, had fallen to extremely low levels of customer satisfaction. People seemed to be working hard, but the client continued to emphasise concern at appalling performance levels. It took six months to turn the contract around to one of the division's highest-performing contracts with great customer satisfaction and a high level of service.

This is how the manager described his success:

> 'It was a question of the perception held by the contract team. We had been taken on to manage the service, but the perception the team had was that they were there to be managed by the client and respond to their wishes. Once I explained the situation to the team they understood that the client wanted them to take a management role. They became more proactive in reshaping the policies and procedures that were hindering performance improvement, and arranged client meetings with the purpose of discussing service management issues rather than defending a poor performance record which had become the norm.'

Team activity is then directed by actual customer expectations rather than by perception. Perception-driven activity is a sure-fire way of wasting valuable resources.

Perception-driven activity is a sure-fire way of wasting valuable resources.

The levels of identity, values, beliefs, capability, behaviour and environment can be used in group problem-solving activities to open up problem space by applying very different perspectives. The more perspectives you can gain on a problem, the more information you will get as to the possible cause. Divergent problems require interventions in more than one area, and so there is always the danger that a solution to one perspective of the problem by itself will not be sufficient to effect the desired change. The 'multiple perspectives' method of problem solving can be adapted to include as many different perspectives as you think are necessary for a particular problem. I will explain the method using the problem types I have mentioned in this chapter.

> **Divergent problems require interventions in more than one area.**

Exercise 9.7: Multiple perspectives

With a large group of 20 or more

Each square in Figure 9.3 represents a room containing a small group of between three and six people. Each room is labelled with a different perspective of the same problem. The groups brainstorm the same problem while remaining within the scope of their allocated perspective. The groups think of the problem 'as-if' it were the type suggested by their allocated perspective. After a period of time each group presents the outcome of their brainstorming session to the whole team.

Most problem-solving sessions will perhaps include, at the very most, five or six different perspectives. However, if a problem is sufficiently diverse and a serious threat to the organisation, all nine perspectives can be included by running the exercise over a number of days and taking, say, three perspectives per session.

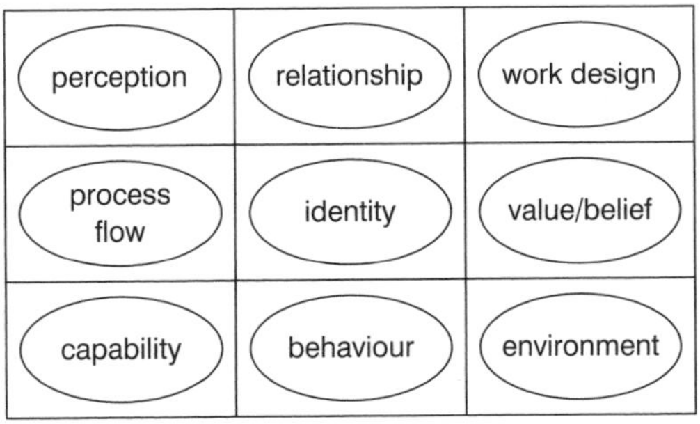

Figure 9.3 Multiple perspectives

With a smaller group

Vary this idea by allocating a different perspective to each member of the group around the same table. Another variation of this method is to use metaprogramme perspectives, i.e. work patterns, activity content, motivational direction, level of activity, attention direction, reference sort, chunk size and group behaviour.

Tips

Participants in this activity will require a thorough education in the whole process, and it will help to provide each group with a reference guide for use while brainstorming. The definitions of each perspective must be clearly stated to avoid confusion between similar components such as 'work design' and 'process flow', 'behaviour' and 'capability'.

The Walt Disney creativity strategy

Walt Disney was perhaps one of the most creative thinkers of our time. His talent for creating animated films transformed the industry and built a hugely successful business empire. His high standards of quality, creativity and perfection were an obsession. His films are a combination of exaggerated character features, stirring music, stories based on human morals and vivid extremes of stillness and action to carry an audience through a range of emotional states. His most famous features include *Bambi* (1943), *Pinocchio* (1939), *Treasure Island* (1950) and *Snow White* (1938), all of which are still shown today on movie screens all over the world.

Robert Dilts, a long-time developer of NLP, has studied the strategies of Walt Disney and produced models for others to use. The underlying thinking style which Disney used to create new characters, stories and film settings was very specific. It consisted of three different phases of thinking:

- Dreamer
- Realist
- Critic

The dreamer

The dreamer phase works purely with imagination, looking for possibilities of what could be. There are no constraints, limitations or evaluations connected to this mode. It is primarily a visual mode with a synthesis of sound and feeling. Disney would visualise symphonic music – giving it form – music being the lead to his preferred visual modality. The physiology associated with the dreamer phase is upright, with the head tilted slightly up and eyes up to the right (visual construct).

The dreamer phase works purely with imagination, looking for possibilities of what could be.

The realist

The realist phase is concerned with the 'how' of implementation – how the output from the dreamer can be put into action and made a reality. It does not seek to evaluate or criticise – rather to explore ways of making the dreamer's vision happen. The key to being an effective realist is the ability to associate with different characters, taking different perspectives on the finer details of the dreamer's vision. To this end it may be useful to adopt the physiology of each character.

The realist phase is concerned with the 'how' of implementation.

The critic

The critic phase is one of detail, logic and consequences. The critic looks for problems using a 'what if' frame. To effectively criticise the work of the dreamer and realist, the critic must be sufficiently removed from the situation. The critic is concerned with getting the details right. Everything must fall into place with no rough edges or unfinished actions.

> **The critic phase is one of detail, logic and consequences.**

This is not a negative stance, but a valuable contribution to checking out ideas and ensuring they meet established criteria and are robust. The critic can be just as creative as the dreamer by identifying a missing or inappropriate element of a plan. Critics should continually ask the question 'what if?' The physiology of the critic is in critical evaluation pose with the head tilted slightly down and the hand to the side of the face or supporting the chin.

Using the strategy

The dreamer does not have a monopoly on ideas. The Walt Disney strategy is a creative process used to generate ideas and each phase is equal in its contribution to creativity. Without a realist and a critic the dreamer's ideas are unlikely to develop into actions. Here are two ways of using the Walt Disney creative strategy in groups.

Exercise 9.8: Disney's perceptual positions

For small groups

This is based upon the same concept of space used earlier in the book, only this time there are four physical locations labelled dreamer, realist, critic and observer. The advantage of setting out physical locations for each perspective is that it helps to separate the different thinking patterns. Try this exercise next time you find

yourself in a meeting where problem, solution and ideas seem
to follow no logical process of thought or discussion. The three
Disney locations ensure that each phase of the creativity process
is separated, and the observer location ensures that they are
working congruently with each other.

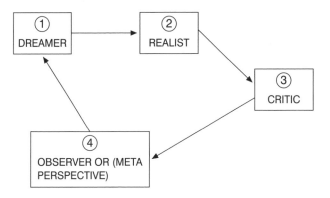

Figure 9.4 Disney's perceptual positions

Step 1

Write a brief description of the context and objective for which
creativity is required. A visual image with the text will help to
keep the group focused on the objectives without having to break
state to read. An image conveys its meaning immediately your eye
catches it while text has to be read before the meaning can be
derived. Hence images will keep a group more focused even while
being observed with peripheral vision.

Step 2

Organise the team into four groups. Ask each group to anchor a
pure and strong state to each of the three locations – dreamer,
realist and critic. If the group is not skilled in anchoring, you can
help them to generate an optimum state for each location by
inviting them to recall a time when they were (a) dreaming, (b)
being a realist and (c) criticising.

Step 3

Associate with each location in turn, starting with the dreamer. Take as much time as necessary to ensure that states are pure before moving on to the next location. In the dreamer location, use visualisation, sound and feelings only. Internal dialogue is not a useful mode for creativity. In the realist location, take the images created by the dreamer and make them work. Associate with any characters that may be involved to get a realistic feel of how they will be affected by the ideas generated. From the critic location, repeatedly ask the question 'what if?' until all the possible problems and dangers have been overcome.

Step 4

Step on to the observer location and consider the whole creativity process happening among the three locations. Check that it is all congruent and focused on the context and objectives.

Step 5

Continue to move through each position until there is satisfaction and congruence with the ideas generated.

A variation for large groups

As an alternative to moving through the perceptual positions, you can have each group remain with one perspective and pass the information around each group. You will need four syndicate rooms for this exercise. In room 1 will be the dreamers who are tasked with generating ideas and passing them to the realists in room 2. The critics in room 3 take the ideas from the realists and pass them to the observers in room 4. The observers do not alter the ideas, but give feedback to each group on how well they are keeping to the context and objectives. They should also recognise and feed back qualitative information about the content of each group's contribution.

A high street chain of stores was investing in a new image and wanted to introduce some creative ideas to attract new customers and keep them in the store for longer. We facilitated managers from different stores through the Disney strategy, first by creating a very playful environment in the room and encouraging crazy ideas. During this process one manager suggested that customers could queue at the checkout in carts that moved along on rails. Many more ideas were generated during the initial dreamer phase.

When it came to the reality stage we set up the room completely differently – we removed the toys and turned the chairs to face the opposite way. It was like everything in the room had been picked up and turned around 180 degrees. We tidied up the mess that had been created during stage 1 and removed materials which were finished with. When we brought the team back into the room we told some stories with a very practical edge to get them into a good 'realist' state. During this stage the 'cart on rails' idea was considered impractical, but another manager came up with the idea of entertaining people in the queue to make the wait more enjoyable. Others chipped in and thought practically about how to make the idea work. At the end of this stage the idea was to let customers in the checkout queue try out products like video games, cameras, hi-tech toys and portable DVD players while they were waiting to be served.

All the ideas that were kept at the end of the realist stage were taken back to the workplace and put to other managers. The final critic stage was held in store so they could see what they had to do to make the ideas work. The 'queue entertainment' idea was implemented and an immediate increase in sales of around 5 per cent was achieved. A key contribution during the critic stage was to make sure plenty of the 'try out' products were held at the till so when the customer arrived at the checkout the product was there to be purchased.

The Einstein strategy

Most people know of Albert Einstein for his Theory of Relativity ($E = MC^2$). Arriving at this formula took Einstein many years. His very first thought on relativity occurred at the age of 16 as he was daydreaming during a maths lesson at school. He wondered what the world would look like if you were sitting on the end of a light beam. And if you were holding a mirror in your hand, would you be able to see your reflection?

Einstein is regarded as a genius for his contribution to science, and we are lucky to have so many historic records that describe his creative-thinking strategy. Here's an example of how Einstein's thinking strategy can be used in a group creativity process.

The technique   Einstein preferred to think in pictures rather than words. Pure visual imagination doesn't have the associations, meanings, rules and structure that a spoken language has. If you think in words, you are already influencing the quality and quantity of ideas which you can potentially generate. Only after thoughts have been generated is the spoken language of any use.

Some people may say that they don't see pictures, or that they don't visualise. What actually happens is that these people do visualise, but they have developed other representation systems in preference to the visual modality. The following is often a convincer for these people: *what I want you to do is imagine a green monkey playing basketball with a purple and yellow hippopotamus. Can you imagine that?* Of course they can. Now, it's time to visualise.

Exercise 9.9: Think like Einstein

The instructions for this are simple. You first need a situation frame – some words that define the problem and perhaps a system diagram showing the problem boundaries. Once the frame is set, people are instructed to think only in visual images. To do so they may need to tame their internal dialogue – tell them that if it creeps in, to turn it off and concentrate on the pictures.

Allow the imagination to take control of the thinking process. Relaxation music will help. Suggest that they may want to relax and close their eyes – whatever is the most comfortable. Sharing ideas as they emerge may stimulate ideas from others in the group. When they have finished invite them to share their ideas with each other freely in small groups of three to five. As each person explains their ideas, the other group members ask questions relating to perception, identity, values and beliefs. For example, what identity would be most useful to carry out this idea? What values and beliefs would be needed to make this happen? What perceptions might people create around this idea?

The results can be documented for later evaluation. This technique can also be used for the dreamer stage of the Walt Disney strategy. Remember that exercises of this nature are designed purely to generate possibilities, and there is no evaluation of ideas at this stage.

"I can never stand still. I must explore and experiment. I am never satisfied with my work. I resent the limitations of my own imagination."
Walt Disney (1901–66), American film cartoonist and director

NLP and procrastination

The ability to avoid certain tasks or decisions is a powerful phenomenon. Just about every manager I have known has owned up to a certain amount of procrastination. The question is: how much time do you spend avoiding doing things that you really ought to be getting on with? If you could stop procrastinating completely, how much extra time would you have on your hands? How much better would you feel at having tackled and completed all the things you have been procrastinating about? So how does procrastination work? Think about a task you need to get done or a decision you are faced with at the moment. As you think about this, how are you representing the thought in your mind? What are your images and sounds like? Is the picture distant, fuzzy or grey? Are the sounds dull and incoherent? What often happens with something you are avoiding is the images and sounds that make up your thinking are distant and grey – this is a function of your unconscious mind. So whenever you think about the thing you feel you should be doing, your mind pushes the thoughts into the distance or background and then moves on to something with more of an instant reward such as making a cup of coffee or checking your email. If there is still time to come back to the task or decision later, you are likely to keep repeating this pattern until the very last minute when the deadline has arrived and you are able to procrastinate no longer. The problem this causes, in addition to the bad feelings of not being in control, is that you have no time for creative input because speed of completion becomes paramount. Sound familiar? Luckily there are techniques to get around this procrastination pattern.

Value to you

Engage only in tasks that mean something to you. If you are unable to find meaning in your work you are probably in the wrong job. It is so easy to fall into the trap of doing work for a living that has no meaning for you, feeling undervalued and then pinning your lack of achievement on poor time management. The result is procrastination. More people than ever today are leaving highly paid jobs because of the lack of personal fulfilment in their role. Of course, like most roles today, there will be some tasks you really enjoy and others you would rather not do – it's the balance that's important. The simple way to check the value content of your work is to keep a record of all the activities you are involved with in a typical week or month, and as you are doing each one rate the value according to what it is doing for you, not for the organisation. How do you feel as you are doing it? What are you getting from it? Which tasks have been causing the most procrastination?

Now take the tasks with the highest degree of procrastination and use one or more of the following techniques to get yourself really motivated to do them. Take one at a time and ask yourself, 'What's important about this task?' If you are unable to find a suitable answer, then maybe it doesn't really need to be done. Or could someone else be doing it instead of you? What would happen if you didn't do it? What could you be doing instead that would be more gainful? Take the tasks that you still feel you should be doing and continue with the next stage of the technique.

Outcome focus

Decide what you want as an outcome for the task. What do you want to have achieved as a result of putting effort into the task? You can use the 'well-formed outcomes' guide in Chapter 3 to make sure you have everything covered. Sometimes procrastination is caused by ill-defined criteria, or a lack of focus on what's really important about the task. Use the following questions to create your 'well-formed outcome'.

1 What do I want to achieve from this?

2 What internal and external resources will I need to complete it successfully?

3 How am I going to get this moving, retain responsibility for whatever happens and stay in control throughout?

4 What will my achieving this do for me and others? What wider impact will it have?

5 How will I know I have been successful? What evidence will I use to measure this?

6 What timescale is realistic and acceptable for me?

Options pattern

Now to the most common cause of procrastination – the options + reactive pattern. If you are motivated by choices and are more reactive than proactive then you are likely to procrastinate whenever a choice is before you. You may be very quick to react when a problem arises, but slow to decide a course of action which has no pressing urgency attached to it. You will recognise this pattern from the tendency to reinvent the wheel, or inertia caused by your reluctance to make a choice. Becoming aware of your options + reactive pattern is the first step to dealing with it. The next step is to decide criteria for each choice you are facing – and then to stick to them! Again, use the following techniques to kick you into action.

Exercise 9.10: Propulsion technique

Think of a time when you really got moving with a task which wasn't urgent and completed it successfully. Notice the imagery that comes to mind and turn up the colours and brightness while bringing it closer until you are fully associated. Now intensify the good feelings and hold them while you continue with the next step.

Take one of the tasks which you have been procrastinating over and create an image of having got stuck in and succeeded. Now create another image of the consequences of having succeeded, and another of you and your new capability now that you have replaced procrastination with action. You now have three images to work with. Turn up the brightness and colour, and see each image clearly inside its own frame. Project the images above the horizon and in front of you. Now, look down and tell yourself (in a determined tone of voice) how you are ready to get stuck in. Look up and merge the three images. See them begin to swirl around and form a spinning orange sphere of dynamic energy. Now move the orange sphere down from your mind into your lower abdomen and spin it faster in a forward spinning motion. Keep telling yourself how you are really ready to get moving … and as the orange sphere spins faster … notice how you are being driven forward ready to act!

Here's another exercise using the orange circle thinking technique, based on an original NLP procedure called collapsing anchors. For this technique you will require a blue pen, an orange pen, a piece of paper, a pair of scissors and some space.

Exercise 9.11: Orange circle thinking

Cut out a square and on it with the blue pen draw a symbol representing what it is you have been procrastinating over. Now place your square on the floor and stand in front of it while feeling what it is like to have been procrastinating over this situation. Now move a few feet away from the blue square, take a couple of deep breaths and answer the following questions:

- What do you want to do with this situation?
- What outcome do you want to have as a result of getting on with it?

■ How do you want to feel, having got it completed?

Now cut out as many circles as you have answers to the above questions, and using the orange pen draw a symbol representing these new ways of responding. Place the circles on the floor at least six feet away from the blue square and stand facing the circles. Bring to mind a time when you did get on with something and achieved a satisfactory and positive outcome. Notice the images you have associated with this time and intensify the colour, brightness and contrast. Bring the image closer to you until the feelings get stronger; then at the peak of intensity turn to look at the blue square and notice how you feel now about that situation. You will have a powerful feeling of wanting to get on with it.

NLP and decision making

How do you know if you are making the best decisions for yourself and for the business? Some say that decision making is intuitive, others that it's the science of weighing up the pros and cons. When you think about having to make a decision, there is always more evidence and experience to help you than you can access consciously. When you have had strong feelings about something and followed through with a decision, chances are you will have achieved a good result. Some people call this intuition. What's actually happening in cases like this is your unconscious mind is having an influence over your thinking. All the experiences you have had that relate to the decision being considered are being drawn upon – too many for the conscious mind to think about. Your unconscious then sends a signal via your feelings advising you whether or not to take the decision. Think of it more as your unconscious intelligence rather than intuition. The trouble is, if you are highly stressed or not a feeling sort of person, you may not sense the signal from your unconscious mind, or you may sense it but ignore it.

One of the causes of poor decisions is that they are often made when you are feeling bad about something. If you think back to some of the better decisions you have made, chances are they will have been made when you were feeling good about yourself. The next time you are facing a decision, make sure you are feeling good about yourself, and if not, choose a technique to change the way you are feeling.

In addition to your unconscious signals you have a decision-making strategy. This consists of the sequence of events inside your mind that you play each time you have a decision to make. You may even use the same decision strategy to order a meal in a restaurant and make a major business decision. If your decision making is not working well, you can improve it or create an entirely new strategy. You may also find that once you have improved your strategy your unconscious signal will become more recognisable to you.

Eliciting your strategy

All strategies are made up of a combination of the following:

- External visual information
- Internal images
- External auditory information
- Internal auditory (such as your internal dialogue and remembered conversations, or the catchy pop-tune you just can't get out of your head)
- Internal dialogue
- External feeling (tactile)
- Internal feelings
- Physiology.

Your strategy will also be influenced by your values, beliefs and metaprogrammes.

Creating a 'good decision' strategy

Think about a good decision you made where you felt it was the right thing to do and where the outcome was positive. Take your mind back to the very first point at which you were aware a decision had to be made. What did you do first? Did you see a picture, have a conversation with yourself or speak to other people? This type of sequence of events has everything to do with the quality of decisions you make. For example, one manager I was coaching had made a series of bad decisions he was very unhappy about. He asked for help to improve the impact of his decisions. During coaching sessions I discovered his 'bad decision' strategy was made up of the following sequence of events:

1 **Internal visual** – mind image of the outcome I want for making this decision

2 **Internal dialogue** – tell self what to do to achieve outcome

3 **Internal feeling** – feels like I really want to decide this now and get something moving.

Notice the sense of urgency to act based on purely internal information – two metaprogrammes possibly responsible for cutting the strategy short. So we spent some time deciding what an improved strategy might consist of and came up with an alternative.

During the session the manager installed the alternative strategy as follows:

1 **Internal visual** – mind image of the outcome I want for making this decision

2 **Internal dialogue** – who could I go to for further information about this?

3 **External auditory** – speak to other people and gather information

4 **External visual** – look for similar examples of this decision being made by others

5 **Internal visual** – revised mind image based on new information

6 **Internal dialogue** – is this enough to go on? If not, return to step 2

7 **Internal feeling** – yes, it feels right, so let's go.

You can use strategies to improve all the key strategy patterns you have, including your strategy for self-motivation, creativity, memory, learning and beliefs. What you are doing here is getting right into the way you put your thoughts together and then creating new choices. Take some time and elicit your strategy for making decisions; then ask yourself if it is working for you or not. If your answer is *no*, then change it.

NLP and presenting to groups

Think of speakers you admire, and of those where you have had to fight to stay conscious as they did their best to send you to sleep. What's the difference? Apart from unique personality traits the one thing that usually separates a dynamic speaker from a dull one is technique and practice. Unless you are naturally gifted you do not become a great speaker overnight. The majority of the top dynamic speakers have worked at it and practised.

Before practice there is an important question to ask: what's the reason for bringing people together in a group? Resist the temptation to ask people to give up valuable time in order to merely impart information to them. This can be done far more effectively by email, letter or brochure. The real opportunity offered whenever people gather for a presentation is to engage them in ideas, both mentally and emotionally. You can engage and inspire your audience by encapsulating many of the NLP concepts and techniques in this book. Bearing in mind that your audience will consist of many different people all with different metaprogrammes, representation systems, beliefs and values, you will have to find a way to accommodate them all if you are going to keep them engaged. Here are some ideas:

1 Decide on your outcome – what is the purpose of your presentation? What message are you trying to convey? Make sure there are no more than three key messages in your presentation. If you are one of a number of presenters at the same event, take time to establish the key messages of the other speakers. Link your messages to theirs by acknowledging their expertise and reinforcing your joint messages.

2 Place a high value on the time people have given up to listen to your presentation. This will ensure that you give the preparation the time and commitment it deserves.

3 Visualise yourself having completed the presentation and doing whatever it is you will do when it is successful – receiving a round of applause, a vote of thanks, some really interesting questions. Keeping hold of this image, use a timeline to determine what it was you had to do to get there. Mark a point on the floor to represent 'now'. Place your outcome together with a symbol to represent what you will see, hear and feel when you are successful on to an orange circle. Walk forward from 'now' to a time when you will have completed your presentation and place it on the floor. Look back to 'now' and enjoy the moment. Then look at all the things you had to do to achieve your outcome for your presentation. Maybe you needed some skills, some research, some time to practise, some professional visuals. Notice at which point on the timeline these things appear, create an orange circle for each one and get a sense of structure for your presentation.

4 Decide what state you want to be in for your presentation and anchor it. Fire the anchor before entering the room (see Chapter 8).

5 Make sure your language is 'artfully vague' and positive (see Chapter 7). At the beginning of the presentation use the 'Yes' set concept. It is generally accepted that if you can get people saying 'yes' three times, you will have them on your side. Make sure that you include everyone in your opening remarks and that they cannot possibly disagree with you for at least three statements. Here is an example:

'Some of you I know will already be familiar with the topic of my presentation this afternoon while for others it will be fresh and new. Either way I know you will all have something to contribute to the debate either now or when you have had an opportunity to reflect. I look forward to and warmly welcome your views and ideas.'

Not much to argue with here and vague enough for everyone to feel comfortable.

6 Include all the predominantly visual, auditory and kinaesthetic people by using predicates in all systems (see Chapter 6). Provide visuals in the form of pictures, photographs and diagrams for the visual people, use voice tone, tempo and speed to full effect for auditory people and make sure that the room is comfortable for the kinaesthetics. Remember that kinaesthetics like to be comfortable in their chairs – they may slouch, cross their arms and possibly fidget. This does not mean they are bored – just comfortable. If possible provide models, toys and samples for them to touch.

7 You can appeal to a number of different metaprogrammes by using body language, gesture and example. Appeal to procedural people by including an outline of what you are going to cover and explain it by listing points on your fingers. Appeal to options people by spreading your arms and suggesting that there may be choices within the points you

raise. As a general rule presentations need to be kept at a high level of language to accommodate everyone – you can satisfy the detail people by pre-framing your presentation and informing them that more detail will be contained in the notes they can collect as they leave. Examples demonstrating your key points will also help to satisfy those with a need for detail.

8 The voice has a range of tone, pitch, resonance, speed and volume. A good presenter will use the whole range of the voice for emphasis. Work the voice with the body posture and gestures to create rich messages for your audience. Make a point of listening to popular presenters and orators and noticing how they use their voice for different effects. Practise changing your voice to reflect the type of emphasis you want. From a deep, loud voice to stress a serious point, change to a softer, quieter voice drawing the audience's attention to a small, specific, but important detail. Explore the range you have available and put together combinations of voice and gesture for greater impact at your next presentation.

9 Use tonal marking to emphasise key words. Use pauses to allow your messages to percolate. Use stories to help with retention – people will remember the story and therefore the meaning of your presentation long after you have finished.

10 If you want to anchor particular states in your audience, then decide beforehand where you want to position yourself for each state. For example, you may wish to stand to the left of the presentation area when anchoring a state of energy and move to the right-hand side when you want your audience to be reflective. You only need to set the anchors a couple of times before the audience will get the idea that as you begin to walk over to the left-hand side you are going to raise their energy levels and vice versa.

11 Speak in everyday language that people will understand

– resist the temptation to use corporate speak. Speak from the heart and believe in what you are saying.

Practise changing your voice to reflect the type of emphasis you want.

Handling questions from the audience

There are three basic requirements for answering all questions:

1 Never answer a question directly until you have determined the intention behind it. This is a distinction about *process*, not content.

2 Be in total uptime when you are asked a question so that your sensory acuity is high, noticing unconscious communication processes in physiology and voice qualities.

3 Remain emotionally detached. If someone has a question – fine. Deal with it. It is the information which is being questioned, not you. If you are asked a direct personal question, it may be better to deal with it after the presentation.

Determining the intention behind the question is quite simple. Sometimes a questioner will provide it for you like this: 'I have just started work in this area and would find it useful to understand more about this subject. What is …?' Others will not be so obliging and will just ask the question, 'Why does x mean that y is unsatisfactory?'

This 'why' question may be straightforward or not – to be safe ask the question, 'Before I explain that for you it would help me to know your level of interest in this area.' The answer to this question will reveal the intention behind the first question, and you will be able to answer more specifically for the questioner.

Some questioners enjoy getting feedback about the nature of their question. These will be the 'externally referenced' people.

You can make them feel OK by saying, 'That's a very pertinent question – thank you for asking it' or a variation of these words.

Hypothetical and judgemental questions

- 'What is your opinion about …?'

- 'What would happen if …?'

- 'How far do you think this can go?'

You can choose a range of responses to these questions, most of which consist of turning the question back to where it came, like a boomerang. For example:

- 'I'm not here to give my opinion but to present the facts. Do you have an opinion you would like to share with the audience?'

- 'That's an interesting idea. Let's see if we can work this out together. If *x* did *y*, what would you expect to happen?'

- 'I don't know the answer to that question. I wonder if anyone in the audience has an answer. Any takers?'

- 'What do you think?'

Questions or statements from confused minds

- 'What did you say the yellow band was for?'

- 'That doesn't fit with what you were saying earlier.'

- 'How can this year's profit be higher than last year's when we all know that sales have taken a downturn?'

You probably want a 'backtrack frame' for these types, and perhaps a 'chunk-up' to a higher level. For example:

- 'Let's go back and cover that once more. I mentioned the idea …'

- 'I'll backtrack and put that into perspective with what I said earlier. The concept of the yellow band …'

- 'Let me explain that by first of all clarifying what I said previously. The overall income for last year ...'

The personal attack

- 'How can middle managers be trusted with this?'
- 'What makes you think engineers will be capable?'

Personal attacks are simple to deal with. You need to direct criticism away from the person and towards the subject matter. Chunking up is also a useful technique. For example:

- 'Trusting is something we all could do more of, and it will be important to trust the procedure designed by the production team.'
- 'This company owes its success to the capabilities of all its employees. They must be continually developed.'

The direct challenge

- 'What is the point of all this?'
- 'I fail to see how this will change anything.'
- 'This has all been tried before – and it didn't work then.'

These questions indicate that the person hasn't bought into your ideas because of a belief they are holding on to. You must decide one of two responses:

1 *Acknowledge the remark/question and move on.* 'I can understand why you have made that statement; however, here is not the most appropriate place to deal with it. I will be happy to talk to you about this after the presentation.'

2 *Shake the belief.* 'That's one perspective on this agenda. Tell me, what do you think the consequences would be of not making a change?' 'What would get you to see it?'

Using your body

Your body is a very useful tool at times in dealing with people who seem to be on ego trips. These people often need to demonstrate to the audience and the presenter that they are experts in your subject. Always avoid getting drawn into a technical debate. Never get defensive. Stick to the process using the techniques explained in this section and for added impact position yourself as closely as possible to the questioner. This will have the effect of putting them under the spotlight which is an uncomfortable place for most people. Using confident gestures at the same time will increase the impact even more.

Dealing effectively with questions is a matter of process. The process consists of the following:

1 Acknowledging the question

2 Identifying the intention behind the question

3 Deciding whether to deal with it now or later

4 Choosing an information frame within which to deal with the question:

- Backtrack

- Relevancy challenge

- Evidence

- Outcome

- Ecology

- As-if

5 Choosing a strategy:

- Boomerang

- Chunking up

- Direct criticism away from person and towards the subject

- Shaking a belief.

"The object of oratory alone is not truth, but persuasion."

Lord Macaulay (1800–59), English historian

The final piece of advice to help you deliver effective presentations is the most important – practise. Just like learning to ride a bicycle, the first time feels a little awkward, and after a while it becomes a habit. Practise by yourself. Watch your physiology in the mirror and record your voice to notice the characteristics. Rehearse your next presentation like an actor would rehearse for a play. After a while, influencing and persuading through the corporate presentation will become quite natural to you. Perhaps you want to choose just one or two techniques to practise for your next presentation. Take it one step at a time.

NLP and motivation

When you are able to fully motivate yourself it will be easier to create the environment for others to do the same. So often I have come across managers asking the same question: 'how do you motivate people?' A good number of these managers are not even motivated themselves. Sometimes they have been feeling stressed and unsure of their role; others have found it awkward just communicating openly with people. I recently heard a human resources director give a presentation to his company of 3,000 people that 'the change we are facing will be very difficult, but we will survive it'. Clearly this director wasn't feeling motivated himself, but worse than this he didn't recognise how his words would impact on everyone else. Survival? How motivating is that?

If you are not fully motivated yourself, work on this, not on other people's motivation. People are very capable of motivating themselves, and as a manager all you need to do is create the environment that makes it easy for them to do so. As you work through the following aspects of motivation, and apply them to yourself, you will gain a better understanding of how to encourage others to do the same.

Aspirations

Motivation can be short term or long term. For example, if I consider cooking and eating an inconvenience to life, and my diet consists of pizza and other fast foods, I will be motivated to eat when hungry, but after a meal I will no longer feel the same urge. However, if my aspiration is to be healthy and nourish myself with good quality food, the motivation to shop, cook, eat and explore healthy options may be a continuous driving force, keeping my kitchen stocked with fresh, healthy ingredients.

When motivation isn't lasting, it could be down to a lack of higher aspiration. This is what truly drives people who show a passion for what they do. Aspirations are bigger than goals. To eat is a goal. To be healthy is an aspiration. Aspirations are more closely related to who you are as a person and what you will be remembered for. An aspiration is something that engages you in activities that make a difference to you or to other people in some way. So, you would not call 'becoming the managing director' an aspiration, but in doing so the aspiration is more about how you can influence other people as the managing director. It is all too common these days for a person to take a job they dislike purely for the financial rewards and perks or personal convenience. When this person becomes a manager they will certainly struggle to motivate others since they do not understand the fundamentals of motivating themselves! Motivation lies not in the rewards of a job, but in the job itself.

Metaprogrammes

When you find it a chore to do a certain task, the chances are you have a metaprogramme conflict. In other words, the task you are doing requires a certain focus that you do not find easy and which may even go against your natural bent – for example, a job requiring attention to fine detail when you much prefer to focus on the bigger picture or a highly procedural task which gives you no opportunity to exercise your preference for options. Metaprogramme patterns can really limit your flexibility in certain situations. Refer to the table on meta-programmes in Chapter 4.

Your metaprogramme preferences that are weighted to one end of the continuum are the ones to be most aware of. If you are happy to work with details just as much as with the big picture, then you have flexibility to do jobs requiring both. Inflexibility arises when you have a strong tendency for one pattern and rarely use the pattern at the other end of the continuum. Metaprogrammes tend to be on a continuum, except for the second pattern 'activity content' where your focus of attention may be shared in varying proportions across the five aspects: people, places, activities, information and things. To engage with tasks that require a metaprogramme you rarely use will cause you to become stressed. When a person finds themselves doing a job that is not aligned with their metaprogramme profile, there is no amount of carrot and stick that will get them performing consistently well. It is far better to fit people to jobs at which they can excel. Of course you can change a metaprogramme pattern; to do so requires the desire to change, a suitable exemplar to model and a technique or two.

How to get fired up!

Now and again I meet people who are so unmotivated they find it a struggle to do anything, even getting out of bed in the morning. This indicates a lifestyle problem and there may be any number of causes behind the lack of drive. You may end up applying a range of techniques to help a person in such a low state, but without a particular subject it is not something a book is best able to deal with.

On the other hand, if you have something specific in mind you really want to do but can't seem to get moving with it, here's a technique to get you fired up and motoring. It could be something you do now but don't look forward to, or something you keep procrastinating over. Perhaps it's a task you tend to get anxious about and don't perform so well. Let's call the thing you want to get motivated about 'X'.

Exercise 9.12: Get fired up!

First of all describe how you feel as you think about X.

Now take a couple of deep breaths and describe how you want to feel instead. As you connect with these positive feelings recall a time when you were feeling this way, and notice the imagery that comes to your mind. If the experience you are thinking of was one where you were highly motivated, the image should be colourful and bright. Notice all the qualities of the image and fix it clearly in your mind. Turn up the brightness, colour, contrast and size of the image to intensify the feelings. Keeping this in your mind, create a new image of you getting on with X in a highly motivated way and have this image adopt the exact same qualities as the first image. Take your image and tilt it towards you slightly while you bring it even closer and feel yourself falling into the image. Now get on with X.

NLP and meetings

NLP can be used to ensure meetings are kept lively, purposeful, focused and above all productive. All too often in organisations we see meetings deteriorating into a set of obligations which people don't look forward to. Meetings are a fundamental function of successful organisations and there is no reason why they can't be kept fresh and lively.

What's the purpose?

It is useful to refer back to the alignment model here. First consider the purpose for holding the meeting. Bear in mind you are asking people to give up valuable (and expensive) time to attend and that they may even have to travel long distances. Is a meeting the best way of achieving your purpose? Would a telephone or video conference be just as effective? Or could you just send them some information? Once clear about your purpose you can set about ways of ensuring people are engaged from the outset. Referring to the alignment model again, encourage people to recognise the role they will play and to consider how they are going to participate. Ask what they want to achieve from the meeting – in other words, encourage them to have clearly defined outcomes. Pre-frame the meeting by highlighting the value for each participant and emphasising the benefits for all when you achieve your purpose. Clear away any doubt that you will achieve your purpose before you begin – even if the purpose is simply to brainstorm some ideas at the outset of a new project.

Accommodate the *in-time/through-time* metaprogramme by having coffee first – this will give the *through-time* people a chance to arrive and exchange niceties and ideas together before the *in-time* people arrive with barely a minute to spare. Neither will miss anything and neither will become frustrated by the other.

Use information frames (see Chapter 7) to keep the meeting on track. Set any ground rules before you start. For example, if you are brainstorming you may want to ban words and phrases such as 'no' or 'that won't work' and make sure even the most outrageous of ideas is included at this stage. This will have the effect of removing reticence and allow people to be free-thinking.

Make sure the environment is conducive to the type of meeting you are holding. If you want people to be creative then you want them looking up a lot, and moving about to break stuck states and create new, more resourceful ones. Sitting down at a table, looking down at papers means that people are naturally in the position of internal dialogue and emotions – this is not conducive to creativity. If possible make sure the room is lit with natural light, allow for frequent comfort breaks and keep the energy moving.

Accommodate visual people with pictures, plans, diagrams, colour, flipcharts, etc. Accommodate auditory people with clear backtracking and analysis, and kinaesthetic people with models, pens or toys to fiddle with, and make sure the seating arrangement is comfortable. Satisfy people who enjoy details by reassuring them they will be needed to put more meat on the ideas once they have been formulated.

Anchors play a big part in meetings and can be either productive or destructive. If participants have had a negative experience at a meeting, they are likely to bring this anchored negativity to the next meeting and may even set up a generalised belief in their minds that 'all meetings are a waste of time' or 'I can never get my point across so what's the point in going?'. You can help to avoid negative anchors by varying the format, environment and content. For example, change the seating arrangement – don't allow people to 'claim' seats – change the venue, vary the time between meetings. Nominate different people to lead the meeting. Create the agenda from real concerns of participants instead of business needs. You may be surprised at the quality of business issues that are presented in this way.

As well as keeping meetings negative-anchor free, you can set positive anchors for people. Begin with an uplifting introduction, even if the last period has not come up to expectation; if you focus on what was good about it you are more likely to set a positive anchor for people than if you open with an ear-bashing. Remember to give an uplifting summary at the end of the meeting that shows what you have achieved during your time together, so that people leave feeling good and wanting to return for the next one.

Use the Meta Model to tactfully get clarity around people's ideas and pace and lead them in their thinking.

NLP and building effective teams

With the ever-increasing focus on team working, leaders need to be on the constant lookout for ways to create and maintain not just *effective* team working but *excellent* team working. The quality of the work achieved will have a direct bearing on the dynamics and effectiveness of the team. A group of individuals makes a team, but they do not necessarily act as a team without active leadership. The team could be considered the basic building block of the contemporary organisation. Each separate team, or building block, is a dynamic force, and their collective efforts are directed at making the organisation successful. Well, that's the idea. Sometimes teams are not given adequate leadership or direction and they can find themselves in a state of dysfunction and at odds with the efforts of other teams.

From an NLP standpoint a group of individuals can be most effective by improving their communication and having a strong sense of identity as a team. In addition to this an effective team will share common values and beliefs about their role and what is possible. The first step to getting your team into this position is to begin open discussion and sharing how each person sees the way things are. From this point you can involve the team in moving forward. In this section there are a number of ideas to help you with this process.

Team performance audit

For teams to work well they must attend to four aspects of being a team. These are as follows:

1 **Team orientation** – the importance of being a team and what this means to each team member

2 **Communication** – the style, content and frequency of communication within the team

3 **Support** – a genuine and sincere desire to help each other succeed

4 **Processes** – how the team makes decisions and solves problems.

The following questionnaire will help your team to measure how well it is doing in each of the four aspects of team working. The results will clearly indicate what the team can do to improve its performance. Give a copy of this questionnaire to each member of your team and explain that the purpose is to gauge how well the team is performing at the job of 'being an effective team'. The result will show what needs to be done to improve. Allow individuals at least 30 minutes to complete the questionnaire and then accumulate the results into the four categories as shown at the end. Feed back the results to the team and ask them to decide what they want to do to improve team performance. Allow up to two hours for this process.

Exercise 9.13: Team performance audit

For each of the 16 statements in the table below circle the answer which best fits with your experience.

	A	B	C
There are sufficient team meetings to review performance	I fully agree	I partly agree	I disagree
I know what the priorities are for me and my team on a day-to-day basis	I fully agree	I partly agree	I disagree
Team values are clear and used as a means of resolving difficult team-related issues	I fully agree	I partly agree	I disagree
The team gets useful feedback from outside the team about the value of its contribution to the business	I fully agree	I partly agree	I disagree
Team members are encouraged to speak openly about problems concerning how the team is working	I fully agree	I partly agree	I disagree
I would feel safe expressing concerns about the team's performance to my team leader	I fully agree	I partly agree	I disagree
Team members frequently update each other on their projects and share work-related information gleaned from around the organisation	I fully agree	I partly agree	I disagree

Communication between my team and key stakeholders who have direct interest in my team's performance works well	I fully agree	I partly agree	I disagree
Team members empathise with and support individuals experiencing work or personal problems	I fully agree	I partly agree	I disagree
Team members positively encourage each other to succeed when tackling difficult challenges	I fully agree	I partly agree	I disagree
Team members coach each other in specific tasks, processes or other technical aspects of their jobs	I fully agree	I partly agree	I disagree
If I were in a dispute with a customer, supplier or another employee I feel confident that my team would support me	I fully agree	I partly agree	I disagree
My team cooperates effectively with other teams inside my organisation	I fully agree	I partly agree	I disagree
The team takes the initiative to brainstorm problems and make improvements to work and/ or team processes	I fully agree	I partly agree	I disagree

Members of my team receive training in creative problem-solving techniques	I fully agree	I partly agree	I disagree
The team takes responsibility for improving its performance on a daily basis	I fully agree	I partly agree	I disagree
Total scores			

Now total the answers you have circled in each column by applying the following scores:

For an answer circled in column A add a score of 1.

For an answer circled in column B add a score of 3.

For an answer circled in column C add a score of 5.

The lowest scoring groups show where development work is needed the most.

GROUP SCORES

Group 1:

Questions 1–4 Team orientation

Score =

Group 2:

Questions 5–8 Communication

Score =

Group 3:

Questions 9–12 Support

Score =

Group 4:

Questions 13–16 Team processes

Score =

Food for thought ...

How does team working in your company compare with that of your competitors?

The impact of values on teams

Some teams and companies invest time and effort creating common values and codes of conduct with the aim of improving the way people cooperate and succeed together. In my experience very few teams seem to have developed the knack of integrating values into their working relationships. The majority end up with a list of heart-warming moral principles on a flipchart and think that that is all there is to it. The consequences of spending time on this activity with poor follow-through can often be seen in a lowering of morale and scepticism the next time someone suggests a 'values creation' day.

If your team or company has embarked, or is soon to embark, upon a journey like this, you might appreciate some tips to help you *live your values* and create real benefits for customers, employees and all stakeholders. I am sure you want the result of your investment in time and other valuable resources to provide the climate for a successful outcome.

Here are some fundamental tips for getting to the outcome you want.

1 Regroup often to revisit your values and find out if they have been upheld, and if so how. A one-off shot is never enough. Get teams together three or four times a year to keep their values alive.

Example: Hold a series of breakfast meetings over the course of a month and focus on one or two values at each meeting. Keep the climate of these meetings informal and encourage the full participation of individuals to be open and honest about the reality of *values* in *action*. Keep the mood positive with a fun element and focus on making improvements to the way values can be used to bring benefits. If your team is dispersed across different time zones hold a video conference. Use available technology to solve time and distance challenges.

2 Keep an eye out for situations in the working environment that compromise your agreed values. Be ruthless with situations that compromise values. If you ignore this, then your values will soon become meaningless and cynicism may set in.

Example: Let's say that you notice a customer sitting in reception for 20 minutes while waiting to be seen by a manager. Do what you can for the customer in that moment, and then be sure to discuss it with your team as soon as possible after the incident. Use the value that has been compromised as a guide to making improvements to the way visitors are received.

3 Use your values when resolving problems or conflicts that occur. Make sure everyone knows which value is being compromised and use the value as part of solution criteria.

Example: Let's say that one of your team values is 'active cooperation with other functions' and you notice that a problem is taking a while to resolve due to a lack of action by someone in your own team. Be open and direct when asking each other, 'How can we use this value to help solve this issue quickly?' Be focused on solutions, not blame or punishment. Use *we* rather than *you and I*.

4 Encourage your team(s) to suggest ways of improving the way values are lived and experienced by others. This will help to increase buy-in to the values and strengthen the impact they have on decision making and conflict resolution.

Example: Emphasise the importance of *living the values* at team meetings, and encourage people to offer experiences where they believe a value has been compromised and where a value has helped to solve an issue. Be 100 per cent committed to taking action in any situation where a value has been compromised.

5 Every now and then, perhaps at an annual conference or seasonal get-together, provide some positive feedback about how your values are being used to resolve everyday situations. This will help individuals to learn how they can put values into action. Tell stories of successes and give recognition to those people who have demonstrated values in action.

Example: Design a series of short workshops and have people working in small groups of say between 8 and 12. The objective is to discuss the experiences in the group of *values in action*, and identify one particular situation that the group feels they want to communicate to everyone else. The situation may or may not be successful; the main aim is to learn from the experience. Encourage each subgroup to choose one situation and create a story to describe it. The next stage is for each subgroup to tell its story to the main group.

You can be very creative with this activity, inviting subgroups to use whatever medium they wish to tell their story, e.g. soap opera, commercial, nursery rhyme, song, drama, mime, or whatever else comes to mind.

"You must be the change you want to see in the world."
Gandhi (1869–1948)

Putting values into action is about what you *do* and what you *say* in the moment that matters. The longer you leave it, the weaker the intervention becomes. Any change requires role models to demonstrate different thinking and behaviour. Anyone who has responsibility for people must recognise the consequences of being a poor role model.

Team leaders and CEOs alike will get great results when they are able to role model the desired change.

People behave as the culture dictates

If an employee lives with fear, he learns to avoid taking risks.

If an employee lives with appreciation, she learns to make an extra effort.

If an employee lives with deceit, she learns to stretch the truth.

If an employee lives with leadership, he learns how to take initiative.

If an employee lives with small expectations, he learns to have limited scope.

If an employee lives with openness, she learns how to be honest.

If an employee lives with a heavy hand, she learns how to beat the system.

If an employee lives with experimentation, he learns how to be innovative.

If an employee lives with ridicule, he learns to keep his ideas to himself.

If an employee lives with formality, she learns to be a bureaucrat.

If an employee lives with mistrust, he learns to be suspicious.

If an employee lives with hostility, she learns to fight.

If an employee lives with indifference, he learns not to care.

If an employee lives with clear values, she learns how to set priorities.

If an employee lives with customer respect, he learns how to deliver outstanding service.

If an employee lives with encouragement, she learns to be confident.

If an employee lives with positive visions, he learns how to perform miracles.

If an employee lives with challenge, she learns how to master change.

Notes

Chapter 1

[1] Ashby, W. Ross, *Introduction to Cybernetics*, Chapman & Hall Ltd, London, 1956.

[2] Bateson, G., *Steps to an Ecology of Mind*, Ballantine Books, New York, 1972.

[3] Semler, R., *Maverick*, Warner Books Inc., New York, 1995.

Chapter 2

[1] Miller, G. (1956), The magic number seven plus or minus two: Some limits on our capacity for processing information, *Psychological Review*, 63, 81–97.

Chapter 7

[1] Grindler, Bandler and DeLozier, *Patterns of the Hypnotic Techniques of Milton H. Erickson, M.D.*, Vols I and II, Meta Publications, 1975, 1976.

Chapter 9

[1] Robert B. Dilts, *Strategies of Genius*, Vol. 2, Meta Publications, 1994.

Index

Adams, Henry B. 4
anchoring 171–4, 175
   collapsing anchors 219
   in meetings 236–7
   process of 172–3
   stimulus 173
   timing 173, 174
Aristotle 50
artfully vague language 141–3, 225
as-if frame 156
associated state 36–7
assumptions 146–7, 149
attention-directed (self-others)
     patterns 80
auditory system 116, 121–3
   anchors 172, 175
   breathing 123
   eye movements 122–3
   gestures 123
   language 122
   submodalities 133
   vocal qualities 123
autopilot 6–7
away from people 77–8, 170

backtrack frame 156–7, 228
behaviour 45
   capability 21–2
   change 3, 24
   culture, result of 245–6
   information from 166
   and language 183
   role models 23
   state dependent 31
beliefs 10, 14–22
   changing 17, 18
   and confidence 17–18
   power of 16–17
   as self-fulfilling prophecies 106
   see also values and beliefs
Bevan, Aneurin 92
body and stress 181–2
body language 114
   presentations 225, 230
Boethius 87
brainstorming 204, 236

Branson, Richard 63
Brown, Gordon 152–3
Butler, Samuel 162

calibration 166
can/can't 7–8, 151–2
capability 21–2
change
   beliefs 17, 18
   levels of 10–11, 12, 24
   pacing and leading 103–5
   resistance to 196
   role modelling 245
   sixth strategy profile table 87–8
   unlearning habits 3
   WIIFM (what's in it for me?)
     102–3
chunk size 80
   chunking down 140–1
   chunking up 140–1, 177, 228, 229
   language 138–41
coaching 107–8
   and enabling 108–11
   questions 108–10
   suggesting 110–11
coercive power 96, 98
collapsing anchors 219
Collins, John Churton 134
communication
   breakdowns 34
   encoding/decoding 27–8
   generative development model 2, 3
   human communication system
     27–8
   information processing 27–8
   levels of 10–11, 12, 24
   NLP model 29, 30–1
   non-verbal 114–15, 165
   surface and deep structure 139
   see also language
comparison sorts metaprogramme 82
complex response 8, 10
conditioning 151
confidence 17–18, 47
congruence 45–7, 159–60
   creating direction 58–9

control-empowerment continuum
98–9
convergent problems 195–6
creativity, group 203–15
    Einstein strategy 214–15
    large group 207, 212–14
    and meetings 236
    multiple perspectives (exercise)
        206–8
    problem definition 204–5
    small group 208, 210–12
    sources of problems 205–6
    Walt Disney creativity strategy
        208–14
creativity, personal 191–202
    anchoring 200–1
    and beliefs and values 194
    blocks, removing 201–2
    convergent problems 195–6
    daydreaming 198
    divergent problems 196–8
    and habitual thinking 192–3
    and innovation 192, 194–5
    language of action 195
    limiting beliefs 194
    scrambling the brain (exercise) 202
    state dependent 200–1
    stepping outside problem 194
    supercharging 203
    thinking on your feet (exercise)
        199
    Walt Disney strategy 198–9
    widening perspective 193, 194
critical submodalities 38–40
culture of organisation
    authoritarian 96, 98
    and employee behaviour 245–6
    learning 96–7, 98
    technical 96, 98
curious response 8–9, 10
cynicism 158–9

daydreaming 198, 209, 214
decision making 100, 162, 199,
    220–3
defeatist response 7, 10
deletion filters 77
detail people 80, 170, 226
direction, creating 58–62
    clear future state 52–8
    congruence 58–9
    corporate mission 53–4

desired future state 63
    feedback 53, 54
    inspirational conductor analogy
        50–1
    integration 62–5
    perceptions of others 54–8
    well-formed outcomes 59–62
Disney, Walt: creativity strategy
    198–9, 208–14, 215
    perceptual positions exercise
        210–14
    phases 209, 210–11
dissociated state 37, 38–9
distinctions, making 22
distractions 75–6, 185
divergent problems 196–8, 206–7
Dobson, Austin 191
downtime 165

ecology 74–5
    and modelling 84
ecology frame 154–5
Einstein, Albert 158, 186, 198
    strategy 214
Emerson, Ralph Waldo 178, 191
emotional distance 184
emotions and memory 34–5
empowerment 92, 93–4
    control-empowerment continuum
        98–9
    definition 93
    disempowering organisations 94
    leadership 106–11
    reframing 105
    and trust 99–100
    see also power
end values 15, 19
environment 23
evidence frame 156
expectations, managing 100–1
expert power 96, 98
externally referenced people 80–1
eye movements 119–20, 122–3, 125
eye-accessing cues 126–7

failure, fear of 70–1
feedback
    incongruence as 46, 65
    learning from 2–3
    on organisational expectations 53,
        54
    sixth strategy state 73–4

filters *see* information filters
flexibility 9–10, 143
future pacing 40, 65

Gandhi, Mahatma 245
generalisations 150
    universal quantifiers 149–50
generative management development
        model 2–3
generative power 96–7, 98
    producing 103, 105
Gibran, K. 64
global people 80
goals 68
    and aspirations 232
    capability 21–2
    and outcomes 59–60
Goethe, Johann Wolfgang von 46
group behaviour (task-people)
        metaprogramme 81
Gurdjieff, George 26
gustatory system 116, 130
gut feelings 46

habit formation 3–4, 6–7
    see also metaprogrammes
habitual thinking 192–3

ideas to action 26–47
    see also creativity; innovation
identity 22
    changes 24
    and confidence 17–18
    creating congruent 75
    identify with your role (exercise)
        12–14
    identity labels 11–14
    mismatch 71–2
    and values and beliefs 20
imagination 26, 191, 215
incongruence 45–7, 160
    identity mismatch 71–2
    in non-verbal communication 115
    unconscious 46
influence 162–3
information filters 29, 30–1
    metaprogrammes 81–2
    see also representation
information frames
    as-if frame 156
    backtrack frame 156–7
    ecology frame 154–5

evidence frame 156
    and meetings 236
    outcome frame 155
    relevancy challenge frame 155
    when handling questions 230
information processing 27–8
innovation 2, 3, 191–5
internal dialogue 126–7
    controlling 131–2
    and decision making 222, 223
    and Meta Model 147–8, 153
    submodalities 130–3
internal representation *see*
        representation
internally referenced people 80–1

Johnson, Samuel 6

kinaesthetic system 116, 123–5
    anchors 172
    breathing 125
    eye movements 125
    gestures and voice 125
    language 124
    submodalities 133
knowledge 21–2

language 32–4, 137
    of action 195
    artfully vague 141–3, 225
    auditory system 122
    and behaviour 183
    chunk size 138–41
    congruence 159–60
    creating reality 33–4
    filtering experience 137–8
    intention 137
    kinaesthetic system 124
    Meta Model 142–3
    Milton Model 141–2, 143
    nominalisations 143–4
    oversimplification 32–3
    as tool 136
    visual system 119–20
    see also communication
law of requisite variety 9
leadership
    empowerment 106–11
    generative development model 2–3
    leader as coaching enabler 108–11
    leader as teacher 106–8
    questioning 108–10

leading 171, 176
learning
    generative 2–3
    levels of 10–11, 12, 24
learning culture 96–7, 98
level of activity metaprogramme 79
liked, being 163–4
limitation strategies 69, 70–1

Macaulay, Lord 231
matching 167–9, 170–1, 175, 176,
    177–8
means values 15, 19
meetings 235–7
    anchors 236–7
    in time/through time people 235
memory 34–40, 138
    dissociating 37
    and emotions 34–5
Meta Model 34, 142–3
    cause and effect 147–8
    comparisons 145–6
    complex equivalence 148
    Gordon Brown's speech 152–3
    lost performatives 145
    mind reading 146–7
    modal operators of necessity 151
    modal operators of possibility
        151–2
    nominalisations 143–5
    presupposition 149
    universal quantifiers 149–50
    unspecified nouns 144
    unspecified verbs 144–5
metaphors 14, 159
    time 182–3
metaprogrammes 29, 76, 77–84
    activity content 78–9
    attention-directed (self-others) 80
    chunk size (global-specifics) 80
    comparison sorts (quantitative-
        qualitative) 82
    group behaviour (task-people) 81
    level of activity (proactive-reactive)
        79
    motivational direction 77–8
    reference sort (internal-external)
        80–1
    relationship filter (match-
        mismatch) 81–2
    work pattern (options-procedures)
        79

Milton Model 34, 141–2, 143
mind reading 146–7, 166
mirroring 167–9, 178
mission statements 53, 150
modelling *see* role modelling
motivation 231–4
    aspirations 232
    creating direction 62–3
    get fired up (exercise) 233–4
    intrinsic 50, 51
    metaprogrammes 233
    motivate yourself (exercise) 186
    and self-mastery 86
    self-motivation 68, 70, 86–7, 217
    sixth strategy state 68–77
    and values 15
motivational direction
    metaprogramme 77–8

negativity 158
nominalisations 143–5
non-verbal communication 114–15,
    165

olfactory system 116, 130
options people 79, 225
Orange Circle Thinking exercise
    219–20
others people 80, 170
outcome frame 155
outcomes
    of employees 107–9
    and goals 59–60
    unclear 75–6
    well-formed 59–62, 107–8, 217–18

pacing 166–71, 178
    extreme neurological states 167
    and leading 103–5, 171
    matching and mirroring 167–9,
        170–1
    matching VAK modalities 170–1
    metaprogrammes 170
    values 169
Pauling, Linus 192
people-focused people 81
perception-driven activity 205–6
perceptual positions
    Disney exercise 210–14
    multiple perspectives 54–8
    perceptual positions (exercise)
        55–8

performance, poor 11, 14
personality profile 19–20
physiology 44–7, 84, 115
power 92, 95–7, 98
  authority 100
  coercive power 96, 98
  empowering people 93–111
  expert power 96, 98
  generating 97–101
  generative power 96–7, 98
  see also empowerment
presenting to groups 223–31
  anchoring states in audience 226
  artfully vague language 225
  body language 225
  gestures 225, 226
  handling questions 227–30
  language 226–7
  VAK predicates 225
  visualising success 224
  voice range 226
  'yes' set concept 225
PRIEST acronym (outcomes) 59–62, 76
proactive people 79
problem solving 205
  see also creativity
problems, responding to 7–10
procedures people 79, 170, 225
procrastination 185, 216–20
  options + reactions pattern 218
  Orange Circle Thinking (exercise) 219–20
  propulsion technique (exercise) 218–19
Pygmalion effect 106

questions, coaching 108–10
questions, handling 227–30
  determining intention 227
  direct challenge 229
  from confused minds 228–9
  hypothetical/judgemental questions 228
  personal attack 229
  strategies 230
  using your body 230

rapport building 104, 114, 164
  pacing 167–9, 171
reaction response 8, 10
reality, map of 28–30

reference sort metaprogramme 80–1
reframing 105, 157–9
relationship filter metaprogramme 81–2
relaxation 31
relevancy challenge frame 155
representation systems 31, 35–6, 115–30
  auditory system 116, 121–3
  gustatory system 116, 130
  information filters 31
  internal dialogue 126–7
  kinaesthetic system 116, 123–5
  lead system 117–18
  olfactory system 116, 130
  preferred system 117
  questionnaire 127–30
  visual system 116, 118–21
resourceful states 37–40, 158
respect and influence 163
role modelling 23, 83–4
  change 245
  and congruence 58, 160

self-awareness 2, 3
self-fulfilling prophecies, beliefs as 106
self-mastery 68–89
self-motivation 68, 70, 86–7, 217
Semler, Ricardo 15–16
sensory information 23, 164–6
  calibration 166
  incongruent signals 165–6
  sensory acuity 165–6
  uptime/downtime 165
sixth strategy state 68–76, 86
  creating (exercise) 72–5
  dislike of task 76
  fear of failure 70–1
  identity mismatch 71–2
  missing skills 84–5
  profile table 87–8
  unclear outcomes 75–6
states of being 34, 45
  associated state 36–7
  calibration 166
  control of 88–9
  dissociated state 37, 38–9
  physiology 44–7
  resourceful states 158
  unresourceful states 34, 36, 37–8, 184–5

see also sixth strategy state
strategies 68–9
    avoidance 86
    limitation 69, 70–1
    sixth strategy state 68–76
stress management 31, 180–2
submodalities 38, 130–3
    auditory 133
    control panel 131, 132
    kinaesthetic 133
    visual 132–3
success 24
    Branson's strategy 63
    visualising 63–5, 188–91, 224
Swish technique 37–40

Tao Te Ching 68
task-focused people 81
tasks
    dislike of 76
    procrastination 185, 216–20
    this not *that* 185–6
teams
    building effective 237–46
    creating direction 51–2
    impact of values 242–5
    performance audit 238–42
thinking 114
    and eye movements 119–20
    internal dialogue 126–7
    and non-verbal communication
        114–15
    reframing 157–9
this not *that* 185–6
time management 182–91
    emotions and priorities 183–4
    focus on what's important
        (exercise) 187
    in time/through time codes 41, 42–3,
        170, 186–7
    planning for success (exercise)
        188–91
    this not *that* 185–6
    time metaphors 182–3
    timelines 41–4, 188–91
        associated/dissociated 41, 42
Total Quality Management 93
towards people 77–8

trust 99, 114, 134
    and influence 163–4
    and liking 163–4

unconscious
    autopilot 6–7
    incongruence signals 46
    influencing thinking 220–1
    and language 138
    non-verbal communication 114–15
    successful behaviour 63–4
unresourceful states 34, 36, 37–8,
    184–5
uptime/downtime 165

values and beliefs 10, 14–22, 31
    end values 15, 19
    group and personal values 169
    identifying your own (exercise)
        20–1
    and identity 20
    means values 15, 19
    pacing values 169
    respecting 101–2
    role modelling change 245
    teams and values 242–5
    value conflicts 71–2
visual system 116, 118–21
    anchors 172
    breathing 120
    eye movements 119–20
    gestures and voice 121
    language 119–20
    submodalities 132–3
visualisation
    divergent problems 198
    Einstein strategy 214–15
    future desired state 63–5
        success 188–91
    presenting to groups 224

Wendell Holmes, Oliver 160
Williams, Raymond 111
words, power of 136–60
work, meaning of 105
work pattern metaprogramme 79

'yes' set concept 225

With the power
of **NLP** you can
sell anything
you want.

HOW TO
SELL
WITH
NLP

PAT HUTCHINSON

9780273735427

HOW TO
COACH
WITH
NLP

ROBBIE STEINHOUSE

9780273738398

With the power
of **NLP** you
can be an
exceptional
coach.

Available from **www.pearson-books.com** and all good bookshops